What do we Know about Jesus?

L. G. Brandon

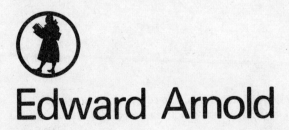

Edward Arnold

First published 1977
by Edward Arnold (Publishers) Ltd
25 Hill Street, London W1X 8LL

ISBN: 0 7131 0095 8

Recycled Paper

Text set in 12/13 pt Photon Times, printed by photolithography,
and bound in Great Britain at The Pitman Press, Bath

Contents

Preface

This book is intended for the use of pupils between the ages of 12 and 14. It aims to present an outline of the story and teaching of Jesus, based upon the documentary evidence of the New Testament, using the accepted methods of historical enquiry.

It recognizes that this evidence has been sifted and analyzed with great rigour during the twentieth century, and that many earlier assumptions have been abandoned by scholars. It asserts that the value of what remains is all the greater because it has survived such a searching examination.

Many pupils come to lessons in Religious Education with the intention of rejecting the information they will be given. Their scepticism is usually based, not upon knowledge, but upon prejudice; and this will increase if they are led to think that all parts of each Gospel are of equal historical value. If they suppose that the story of the miracle at Cana is just as important as the story of Easter, and dismiss the one as incredible, they may well reject the other without examining the evidence. This book asks them to study parts of the New Testament in the ways in which any other historical 'source' material is examined, and it tries to include no assumptions or judgments which will have to be abandoned if the pupils attempt more advanced study.

Most Bible extracts have been taken from the New English Bible.

It is hoped that the text, questions and illustrations will provide ample material for pupils who are working at different speeds. Most of the questions are intended to be within the range of pupils of average ability, but a few are likely to require some preliminary discussion in class.

Acknowledgements

New English Bible 2nd edition © 1970 quoted by permission of Oxford and Cambridge University Presses.

The publisher would like to thank the following for permission to use copyright photographs:

Aspect Picture Library (52), Focus 4 (55), French Government Tourist Office (64), Israel Government Tourist Office (2, 61, 67), Lucas Aerospace Ltd (58), National Gallery (10, 50, 96, 100), Paul Popper Ltd (18, 20, 37, 41, 80), Ronald Sheridan (11, 22, 48).

1 How do we know about Jesus?

Simon Peter, the fisherman from Galilee, waited in Jerusalem, not knowing what to do. His mind was in a muddle: everything had gone wrong.

His master, Jesus, from whom he had expected so much, had been tried and executed, charged with saying wicked things about God.

Peter, confused and scared, had told people that he had never known Jesus, and he was ashamed of himself. All the fine hopes of the last few months had ended in disgrace, for Jesus and for himself. It had all been a sad mistake.

Two days later, certain women, friends of Jesus, went to his tomb, came back hurriedly, and said that it was empty. Peter may have gone to look for himself, but whether he did or not, he was no happier than before. He knew that the body might have been stolen: and wherever it was, Jesus was still dead.

Not long afterwards, Peter heard the voice of Jesus. There was no doubt about it: Jesus was talking to him, and Peter could see Jesus. The impossible had happened. Jesus, who had died, was no longer dead. Nothing would ever be the same again.

Peter spent the rest of his life telling the world about Jesus Christ, who was alive after death.

1

The oldest known account of these events is in a letter which Paul wrote to the Christians in Corinth, just over twenty years later. He told how Jesus:

> 'appeared to Cephas [Peter], then to the twelve [disciples]. Then he appeared to more than five hundred brethren at one time, most of whom are still alive, though some have fallen asleep. Then he appeared to James, then to all the apostles [men sent out to preach]. Last of all ... he appeared also to me.'
>
> (*I Corinthians 15, verses 5–8*)

Jerusalem as it is today showing the Jaffa Gate

From this account, and from others, we know that the disciples and friends of Jesus were completely certain that they saw him, spoke with him, and even ate with him. They knew, now, that Jesus had not been silenced by a human death, and that he was the Messiah, the greatest of all leaders, for whom the Jews had waited for so long. (The Jews believed that the Messiah would lead them so well that they would be able to live as God had always wanted them to do. Sacred oil would be sprinkled on the head of the Messiah, so that he would be 'The anointed one' (*see page 18*). This is the meaning of the Greek word 'Christos', or 'Christ').

If Jesus was the Christ, the Messiah, all Jews must be told about him, and perhaps all other people also. For some of the disciples and friends of Jesus, this became the main work of the rest of their lives.

Wherever they went they announced that Jesus, the Christ, was alive, and they spoke of the things he had done and of the stories he had told.

At first they felt that they must spread their message in a great hurry, because they thought that it would not be long before Jesus appeared again, to finish his work. Their preaching was successful, and groups of believers were formed in Palestine and the lands to the north, in Greece, and even in Rome.

The months and the years went by, and they began to realise that Jesus might not come again while they were still alive.

It seems that during these early years nobody attempted to write down what Jesus had said. There was no time for that. His stories and his sayings were repeated, time and again, by men who were well-trained in learning things by heart, but it was natural that some of the details should become altered a little in the telling.

Much of the teaching of Jesus had been given in the form of parables, which were stories about very human characters. But usually Jesus had left his hearers to work out for themselves what message he had meant these stories to give. As the preachers explained the messages, they may have misunderstood what Jesus had intended. But they had no doubt that Jesus had spoken about God in ways which were quite new.

The word 'tradition' means a message which is passed on by word of mouth, but not written down. Therefore, we call the stories and sayings of Jesus which were repeated during these years the 'tradition' of the Early Christian Church.

Sometimes, Bible scholars, using all possible clues, can suggest the actual words which were used when a parable or a story was repeated in the 'tradition'. If they can do this, they know that they have come as close as it is possible to be to the words which Jesus actually spoke. They try to do this mainly by the very close study of the Gospels of Matthew, Mark, Luke and John.

A **Gospel** is a 'God-story', or a 'telling of good news'. The probable dates of our Gospels are:

> Mark: about 65 AD
> Luke and Matthew: between 70 and 90 AD
> John: a little later.

Mark may have known Peter well, but this is not certain. Luke, who also wrote **The Acts of the Apostles**, travelled with Paul on some of his missionary journeys.

There is no clear proof of who wrote the Gospels which are named after Matthew and John.

We know that at least five other Gospels were written, but large parts of these have been completely lost.

It seems that in the years after 50 AD some of the stories and sayings of Jesus had been written down, perhaps as a help to new preachers. The gospel-writers used some of these written collections, and some scholars believe that Matthew and Luke also took much of their material from Mark.

The gospels were not written to tell the life-story of Jesus, and they do not describe what he looked like. Each was written for Christians and others who lived in a certain area: for example, Mark probably wrote for a group in Rome.

The purpose of each gospel was to show that Jesus was alive after death, and to drive home his teachings about God. Each writer selected the stories and the teachings which he thought the most important, and arranged them in the way which seemed to give their message most clearly. We may wish that, instead, he had given the stories and sayings as he had first heard them or read them: and our scholars can sometimes suggest how they may have been worded in the early days, before they were written down. In this way the scholars may bring us nearer to the people who saw and heard Jesus during his lifetime.

Where this cannot be done, we have to rely upon the words of the gospels. But these were not written for us, and there are many things which we would like to know, and are not told.

We cannot paint an accurate portrait of Jesus, and we cannot write a full account of his life. But we *can* know what he taught, and what he felt for people in trouble.

Above all, we know that the events of the first Easter-time so revived and inspired his heart-broken followers that they 'turned the world upside down'. (*Acts 17, verse 6*)

Questions

1 When did Peter deny that he had known Jesus? (*See page 7.*)

2 Why did the news of the empty tomb not revive Peter's spirits?

3 At the beginning of his Gospel, Luke wrote: 'Many writers have undertaken to draw up an account of the events that have happened among us, following the traditions handed down to us by the original eyewitnesses and servants of the Gospel.'
What can we learn from this?

4 How do we know that all the many thousands of pictures of Jesus are based only upon guess-work?

Problems about dates

At the time when the Gospels were written, the Romans gave each year the name of the reigning emperor, and a number. The first year of Augustus was followed by the second year of Augustus, and so on.

Luke wrote that Jesus was born in the reign of Augustus, and Matthew added that it was during the reign of Herod, the Roman governor of Palestine, but we do not know in which year of Augustus or in which year of Herod.

About five centuries later it was decided to re-number all the years since the birth of Jesus so that the names of emperors and kings could be dropped. Instead, each year was numbered as a year 'of the Lord' (Anno Domini), so that 500 AD meant 500 years after the birth of Jesus. Earlier years were numbered as years 'Before Christ' (BC).

Unfortunately, mistakes were made, because, according to the new numbering, Herod died in 4 BC. But Jesus was born before Herod died, so we have to make the strange statement that Jesus was born in 4 BC or earlier.

Luke wrote that John the Baptist began his work in the 15th year of the emperor Tiberius, and this was either 28 AD or 29 AD. Jesus began his public teaching soon after this, and Matthew, Mark and Luke suggest that he was crucified after little more than one year. But according to John, Jesus taught for about three years. Therefore we cannot be certain about the date of the Crucifixion. It may have been as early as 29 AD or as late as 33 AD.

The dates when the Gospels were written cannot be fixed exactly. (See page 44).

2 The boyhood of Jesus

Jesus grew up in the small town of Nazareth, 1,100 feet above sea-level, in the hilly district of Galilee.

Galilee was separated from the rest of Palestine by Samaria, whose people were hated by the Jews (*see page 44*).

Many of the people living in Galilee were not Jews, and some of them spoke Greek; but it seems that Jesus spent most of his time among the Jewish people.

The language of the Jewish scriptures was Hebrew, which Jesus learnt to read; but this was no longer used in everyday life. It had been replaced by Aramaic, and this was the language which Jesus spoke.

Although the Gospels were all written in Greek, a few of the words of Jesus were given in Aramaic. (*See page 20.*)

Possibly Jesus spoke with a strong Galilean accent. Peter, his fellow-countryman, certainly did so, since Matthew tells us that while Jesus was being questioned by the High Priest (*see page 88*).

'Peter was sitting outside in the courtyard. And a maid came up to him and said, "You also were with Jesus the Galilean." But he denied it before them all, saying, "I do not know what you mean." And when he went out to the porch, another maid saw him, and she said to the bystanders, "This man was with Jesus of Nazareth." And again he denied it with an oath, "I do not know the man." After a little while the bystanders came up and said to Peter, "Certainly you are also one of them, for your accent betrays you." Then he began to invoke a curse on himself, and to swear, "I do not know the man." And immediately the cock crowed. And Peter remembered the saying of Jesus, "Before the cock crows, you will deny me three times." And he went out and wept bitterly.'

(*Matthew 26, verses 69–75*)

As Jesus grew, the family of Mary, his mother, became quite large. We know this because, when he returned to Nazareth, many years later, people asked: 'Is not this the carpenter, the son of Mary and brother of James and Joses and Judas and Simon, and are not his sisters here with us?'

(Mark 6 verse 3. *The rest of what was said is given on page 59*).

It is because of this extract that we think that Jesus was trained as a carpenter. But this is not quite certain, because in Matthew, chapter 13, verse 55, the people ask: 'Is not this the carpenter's son?' They do not suggest that Jesus, also, had been a carpenter.

Questions

1 What language did Jesus speak?

2 What other language could he read?

3 How did people know that Peter came from Galilee?

4 How did Peter deny Jesus three times?

5 How do we know that Jesus had more than one sister?

The visit to Jerusalem

Once every year, the Jews held the Feast of the Passover, in memory of the time when the Hebrew slaves had been brought out of Egypt. The Jews believed that the slaves had been allowed to go because a mysterious death had struck the eldest children in Egyptian houses, but had *passed over* the houses of the Hebrews.

When Jesus was twelve years old, his parents took him to the Festival of the Passover in Jerusalem, a journey of at least 70 miles. They probably travelled much further than this, in order to avoid crossing Samaria.

The story is told in Luke 2 verses 41–51.

> 'Now his parents went to Jerusalem every year at the feast of the Passover. And when he was twelve years old, they went up according to custom; and when the feast was ended, as they were returning, the boy Jesus

Map of the Temple at the time of Jesus

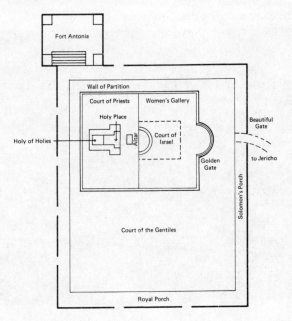

stayed behind in Jerusalem. His parents did not know it, but supposing him to be in the company they went a day's journey, and they sought him among their kinsfolk and acquaintances; and when they did not find him, they returned to Jerusalem, seeking him. After three days they found him in the temple, sitting among the teachers, listening to them and asking them questions; and all who heard him were amazed at his understanding and his answers. And when they saw him they were astonished; and his mother said to him, "Son, why have you treated us so? Behold, your father and I have been looking for you anxiously." And he said to them, "How is it that you sought me? Did you not know that I must be in my Father's house?" And they did not understand the saying which he spoke to them. And he went down with them and came to Nazareth, and was obedient to them; and his mother kept all these things in her heart.'

'Christ disputing with the Doctors' by Preti

Modern Jewish pilgrims at Passover time

Questions

1 For how long had Mary and Joseph travelled on the return journey before they missed Jesus?

2 Does this suggest that they travelled with a large party or with a small one?

3 Did they find Jesus at once in Jerusalem?

4 Where was he found?

5 Jesus was listening and asking questions. What else was he doing?

6 When Jesus called the temple 'my Father's house', what did he mean?

7 Why did Mary and Joseph not understand this?

8 According to the last sentence of the extract, did Jesus normally give any trouble at home?

9 What is meant by 'his mother kept these things in her heart'?

It was not surprising that Mary and Joseph were puzzled, and we know that it was a long time before they and their other children realized who Jesus really was.

The Eastern Mediterranean at the time of Jesus

3 The Chosen People and the Messiah

The Chosen People fail

The Hebrews believed that since the time of Abraham they had been the Chosen People of their God (Yahweh). Yahweh had chosen them to do his work in the world, and they knew that because of this they must live as Yahweh wished them to live. They must obey the Ten Commandments, and all his other laws.

After Moses had rescued the Hebrews from slavery in Egypt, and Joshua had led their children into Canaan (Palestine), they ran into so much trouble that they wondered whether Yahweh had forgotten the promises made to Abraham, Jacob and Moses. From time to time they worshipped other gods, and prophets (great teachers) such as Elijah warned them that there would be more punishment from Yahweh because they had deserted him.

For a time, things were better, but in 597 BC and again in 586 BC the Jews were taken into Babylonia, after Jerusalem had been captured.

Later, the Babylonians were conquered by the Persians, and from 538 BC onwards, many thousands of Jews were allowed to return to Palestine. But they were still under Persian control. Later they were ruled by Greeks (from 331 BC to about 165 BC), and then, after a long period of comparative freedom, they were conquered by the Romans.

So, when Jesus was born, the Jews had been under foreign rule during many centuries. But they had always believed that at last they would have their own king. They expected that he would come from the family of King David, and that he would be a wonderful ruler, who would free them from their foreign conquerors. They spoke of him as 'the anointed one', because oil would be sprinkled on his head, as a sign that he was working

Anointing a king

for God. This is one important meaning of the name *Messiah*, which was later used for him.

During the two centuries before Jesus was born, many Jews thought that the Messiah would be much more than a great king. They now believed that Yahweh was not just the greatest of many gods: they believed that he was the *only* God, and therefore the God of all people in the world. They believed that God had chosen the Jews to tell all people about Him, but that they had failed to do this properly. Therefore He would send the Messiah to give one last chance for all people to learn about God. Then the Messiah would act as a judge, and the world would come to an end. People who had obeyed God faithfully

Map of Palestine at the time of Jesus

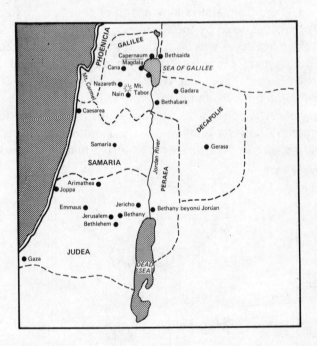

would live on, in great happiness and glory, under the 'Rule of God'. The others would be punished, for ever.

Thus, before the time of Jesus, there were two different ways of thinking about the Messiah. For some, he was to be a great conquering king: for others, he was to be a man sent by God to show people how they might be saved from a terrible punishment.

Many people thought that God would send Elijah back to earth as a messenger to announce the coming of the Messiah. (We are told in the Second Book of Kings, chapter 1, verse 8, that Elijah 'wore a garment of haircloth, with a girdle of leather about his loins'.)

Note. Names used for 'the anointed one' in the Jewish scriptures were: Son of David, Son of Man.

Exercise

Complete these sentences. Each blank stands for **one** missing word.

1 The Hebrews called their God . . . . .

2 . . . . . rescued the Hebrews from . . . . .

3 . . . . . warned the Hebrews that . . . . . would punish them for deserting him.

4 Between 586 BC and 538 BC most Jews lived in . . . . .

5 In the centuries before Jesus was born, the Jews were under the rule of . . . . and . . . . .

6 'Messiah' means . . . .

7 Many Jews thought that the Messiah would come from the family of King . . . . ., and would free them from their . . . .

8 Other Jews thought that the Messiah would be sent to give all . . . . . one last . . . . . to learn about . . . . . before the world came to an . . . . .

4 John the Baptist

The Jews believed that they were near to God in lonely places, and they would think it quite natural that a new religious leader should begin his work in the wilderness or desert.

They had read in *Isaiah 40 verse 3:*

'A voice cries: "In the wilderness prepare the way of the Lord, make straight in the desert a highway for our God." '

Mark altered the wording of this passage so that it seemed to prophesy the coming of John the Baptist:

Mark 1 verses 2–6

'As it was written in Isaiah the prophet, "Behold, I send my messenger before thy face, who shall prepare thy way; the voice of one crying in the wilderness: Prepare the way of the Lord, make his paths straight—"

John the baptizer appeared in the wilderness, preaching a baptism of repentance for the forgiveness of sins. And there went out to him all the country of Judea, and all the people of Jerusalem; and they were

16

baptized by him in the river Jordan, confessing their sins. Now John was clothed with camel's hair, and had a leather girdle around his waist, and ate locusts and wild honey.'

Note 'Locusts' was another name for pods from the carob tree. However, many experts believe that 'locusts' refers to the insect, which is still eaten by poorer people in the Middle East today.

Here is an example of the teaching of John the Baptist.

Luke 3 verses 10–14

'And the multitudes asked him, "What then shall we do?" And he answered them, "He who has two coats, let him share with him who has none; and he who has food, let him do likewise." Tax collectors also came to be baptized, and said to him, "Teacher, what shall we do?" And he said to them, "Collect no more than is appointed you." Soldiers also asked him, "And what shall we do?" And he said to them, "Rob no one by violence or by false accusation, and be content with your wages." '

People wondered if John was the Messiah, but all four Gospel-writers make it plain that John denied this:

"I baptize you with water; but he who is mightier than I is coming, the thong of whose sandals I am not worthy to untie; he will baptize you with the Holy Spirit and with fire."

(*Luke 3 verse 16*)

Exercise

1 The Jews thought that they were near to God in . . . . . places.

2 According to Isaiah, the 'highway for our God' was to be made in the . . . . .

3 The clothes of John the Baptist were like the clothes of
. . . . .

4 John told the people that they must share their . . . . . and
their . . . . .

5 John said that he was not the . . . . .

The baptism of Jesus

Mark tells us (*Mark 1 verses 9–11*):

> 'In those days Jesus came from Nazareth of Galilee
> and was baptized by John in the Jordan. And when
> he came up out of the water, immediately he saw the
> heavens opened and the Spirit descending upon him
> like a dove; and a voice came from heaven, "Thou art
> my beloved Son; with thee I am well pleased." '

The River Jordan

The four Gospels all refer to the baptism of Jesus, but there are several questions which cannot be answered with certainty.

1 Was it Jesus who saw the dove and heard the voice? The Gospel of John (John 1 verse 32) says that the Baptist declared that he saw the dove.

2 Did John the Baptist know that Jesus was the Messiah? The Gospel of John is quite certain that he did (John 1 verse 34). Yet Luke tells us that some time later, John sent men to Jesus asking, 'Are you the one who is to come, or are we to expect some other?' (Luke 7 verse 20).

3 Why did Jesus wish to be baptized? John required men to confess their sins: did Jesus have any sins to confess?

The Gospel-writers found this an awkward question, and Matthew explained that John did not wish to baptize Jesus, but that Jesus said that he was obeying the will of God. (Since all four Gospels included an awkward story, we can feel certain that the baptism really occurred).

4 Did Jesus, at his baptism, begin to believe that he was the Messiah? We cannot be certain, because the Gospel-writers were unable to know what Jesus was thinking. Also, we cannot be sure that Jesus ever spoke of himself as the Messiah. (See page 74).

Questions (more difficult)

1 The first of the Ten Commandments was: 'You shall have no other gods before me.' How does this suggest that there was a time when the Hebrews thought that there were other gods besides Yahweh?

2 When (in Luke 7) John the Baptist sent men to see Jesus, what was the meaning of the question they asked him?

3 How might the story of the baptism of Jesus suggest that he had sins to confess?

4 Why was the story of the baptism of Jesus a difficult one for the Gospel-writers to tell?

5 If the Gospel-writers had not been certain that Jesus had been baptized by John, why might they have been glad to leave this story out?

6 Luke says that John began to baptize 'in the fifteenth year of the Emperor Tiberius'. This year was probably 28 AD or 29 AD. About how old was Jesus when he was baptized?

The Jordan valley

5 Jesus thinks about his work

After his baptism, Jesus needed time to think about his life's work, and he needed to be alone.

Mark tells us simply:

> 'Thereupon the Spirit sent him away into the wilderness, and there he remained for forty days tempted by Satan. He was among the wild beasts; and the angels waited on him.'
> (*Mark 1 verses 12–13*)

The Jews believed that the wilderness was the home of evil spirits, but they also thought that it was a place where a man could be near to God. The angels of God could guard him and supply him with food; and if the wild beasts were friendly, this was a reminder of the happy days of the old story of the Garden of Eden.

'For forty days' means 'for quite a long time'. Mark knew, then, that Jesus had spent many days alone, thinking about the future, and that this had been a very difficult ordeal, because he had been 'tempted by Satan'.

21

The wilderness of Judea

Matthew and Luke add much more detail. They say that Jesus had nothing to eat throughout the period, and that the worst trials came at the end of the time.

How did they know this? Jesus had nobody with him in the wilderness, and yet the Gospels describe conversations between Jesus and the devil or, as we would say, they describe thoughts which troubled the mind of Jesus. Obviously, nobody but Jesus could have known of these thoughts, and so it is most likely that Jesus told his disciples about them later.

Perhaps these were the thoughts:

'If I am the Messiah, am I to use the powers of God simply to give people all the good things they want (which is what they expect from the Messiah)?

Am I to be a conquering king who will free the Jews from foreign rule?

Would it be right for me to prove, once for all, that I am the Messiah, by putting myself in great danger, so as to find out whether God will save me from harm?'

Jesus found his answers in the Jewish scriptures, showing how well he had read them.

The answers were:

1 Men need much more important gifts than earthly goods. Also, it is God who gives us bread, and even the Messiah must not try to take the place of God.

2 The Messiah cannot be a conquering king without doing some things which are evil, that is, things which would involve working for the devil.

3 It would not be right for the Messiah to *test* the powers of God, because this would show that he did not fully trust God, but needed to try an experiment to see whether God would carry out a promise.

All these suggestions are based upon the accounts given in *Matthew 4 verses 1–11* and *Luke 4 verses 1–13*. Here is Luke's story:

> 'Full of the Holy Spirit, Jesus returned from the Jordan, and for forty days was led by the Spirit up and down the wilderness and tempted by the devil.
>
> All that time he had nothing to eat, and at the end of it he was famished. The devil said to him, "If you are the Son of God, tell this stone to become bread." Jesus answered, "Scripture says, 'Man cannot live on bread alone.' "
>
> Next the devil led him up and showed him in a flash all the kingdoms of the world. "All this dominion will I give to you," he said, "and the glory that goes with it; for it has been put in my hands and I can give it to anyone I choose. You have only to do homage to me [bow down to me] and it shall all be yours." Jesus answered him "Scripture says, 'You shall do homage to the Lord your God and worship him alone.' "

The devil took him to Jerusalem and set him on the parapet of the temple. "If you are the Son of God," he said, "Throw yourself down; for Scripture says, 'He will give his angels orders to take care of you', and again, 'They will support you in their arms for fear you should strike your foot against a stone.' " Jesus answered him, "It has been said, 'You are not to test the Lord your God.' "

So, having come to the end of all his temptations, the devil departed, biding his time.'

The devil was biding his time, waiting for another chance to put Jesus to the test. This suggests clearly that there were other times when Jesus had to make painful decisions, refusing to do what people expected him to do, because what they wanted was against the will of God.

It is more than likely, also, that Jesus knew that he would be obliged to suffer a cruel death, and there may have been many times when he felt desperately anxious to avoid this, if he could. These, too, would be times of ordeal or 'temptation'.

Perhaps Matthew and Luke describe thoughts which came to Jesus on many different occasions, but put them together into one story. But the message is clear: Jesus knew that he could not be the sort of Messiah whom most Jews wanted.

Questions

1 What words of Luke show that he thought Jesus did not camp in one place in the wilderness?

2 Jesus was shown all the kingdoms of the world 'in a flash'. Which is the most likely meaning:
  a that he saw a map of the world?
  b that he stood on a very high mountain, looking at distant views?
  c that he formed a picture of the kingdoms in his mind?

3 A man who does 'homage' to another man becomes his servant (his 'man'). Why might Jesus think that if he became a conquering king he would have to serve the devil?

4 If Jesus had put himself, deliberately, into great danger, how would he have been *testing* God?

5 What is the meaning of 'biding his time'?

6 The answers which Jesus gave came from the Book of Deuteronomy 6, verse 13 and verse 16; and chapter 8, verse 3. Find these verses in your Bible, and say which verse Jesus used for each temptation.

7 On page 24 you are told that Jesus had to make 'painful decisions', was 'put to the test', and went through 'times of ordeal'. Luke refers to all these occasions as times of
. . . . .

A synagogue

6 Jesus begins to teach

Mark writes that Jesus began to teach in Galilee when he heard that John the Baptist had been put in prison by Herod Antipas, the governor of Galilee. (Herod had married the wife of his brother, Philip, while Philip was still alive, and John had said publicly that he had broken the laws of God. The story is told in Mark 6 verses 17–29.)

Often, Jesus taught in the 'synagogues' or churches in the towns which he visited. Services were held in them on the Sabbath (Saturday) and on the days of special festivals. There were prayers, hymns of praise, and readings from the books of the

26

A rabbi

Law (the first five books of our Bible) and from the Jewish prophets. The readings were then explained by 'rabbis' (teachers) and by 'scribes' (men who had make a special study of the scriptures). Some scholars think that Jesus may have been a rabbi.

Rabbis and scribes were not priests. Priests carried on their duties in the Temple of Jerusalem, offering the daily sacrifices of a lamb at daybreak and another in the afternoon. For Jews, the Temple was the most important of all buildings, but their regular worship took place in the synagogues.

When Jesus taught, in synagogues or in the open air, he told people that they must always think of God as their Father, and that they must talk to Him as a child talks to his earthly father, trusting and respecting Him completely, but feeling very close to Him, and knowing that He has an unbounded love for his children.

He told the Jews to speak to God as 'My Father', using **Abba**, a homely word, which children learnt easily. This was instead of the type of prayer which was often heard:

> Blessed art thou, Yahweh
> God of Abraham, God of Isaac and God of Jacob
> the most high God
> Master of heaven and earth.

'Abba', for God, was something quite new and disturbing, especially as Jesus said that God loved all His children: even those who were so wicked that no law-abiding Jew would have anything to do with them.

In all his teaching Jesus returned again and again to one central message. Jews believed that a time would come when all people who had served God faithfully would join Him in happiness and glory (*see page 15*). Jesus said that the time had now come. All who listened to him and accepted his challenge could learn what God wanted them to do: and through doing the will of God they could receive all the gifts which God had promised.

It is not easy to grasp the full meaning of this message. The words of Mark are:

'The kingdom of God is upon you,' meaning: 'It is already here', or 'It is very near.'

'Kingdom', in everyday language, means 'a country ruled by a king', but Jesus certainly did not use an Aramaic word which meant just this.

We may get nearer to the meaning if we think of the 'rule'

of a king by which we mean all the ways used by the king to keep his people in order and to look after their interests. Using the word in this sense we can understand the message as meaning:

'The time of the rule of God is upon you.'

It is certain that Jesus told his hearers that they had no time to lose: they must make up their minds at once, and either accept his challenge or refuse it. If they accepted, they would be at once under the rule of God, and would show it by the way in which they lived.

But Jesus also spoke as if the full glory of the rule of God would not be known until later. In one sense it could be known at once: in another sense it would be known, fully, only in the future.

Some parts of the teaching of Jesus are not easy to understand, and one reason for this is that his Aramaic words have been translated into Greek and then into English. But clear and vivid pictures come from the stories which he told about the people among whom he lived. There are forty-one of these 'parables', and from them we can learn how God wants men to respond to his love, and how strongly Jesus drove home the challenge that men must decide at once about his message.

Questions

1 Who put John the Baptist into prison?

2 How often were services held in synagogues?

3 What name was given to men who made a special study of the scriptures?

4 In what building did priests carry out their work?

5 What was the meaning of the Aramaic word 'Abba'?

6 When Jesus spoke about the love of God, what was it which disturbed law-abiding Jews?

7 In which Gospel do we read: 'The kingdom of God is upon you'?

8 What does 'upon you' mean?

9 What is meant by:
a the kingdom of King Henry VIII?
b the rule of King Henry VIII?

10 In what two different ways did Jesus speak about the rule of God?

11 From what language have our English Gospels been translated?

12 How many of the parables of Jesus can be found in the Gospels?

7 Parables

The prodigal son and his father

Jesus invited everybody to learn from him about the love which
God gives to his children, but many respectable Jews were
shocked at the way in which he behaved. They thought that he
ought to choose his friends more carefully, and that it was quite
disgusting that he should eat with tax-collectors and with other
men who were thought to be dishonest in their work. Jesus told
this story (*Luke 15*):

> 'There was once a man who had two sons; and the
> younger said to his father, "Father, give me my share
> of the property." So he divided his estate between
> them. A few days later the younger son turned the
> whole of his share into cash and left home for a dis-
> tant country, where he squandered it in reckless
> living. He had spent it all when a severe famine fell
> upon that country and he began to feel the pinch. So

31

he went and attached himself to one of the local land-owners, who sent him on to his farm to mind the pigs. He would have been glad to fill his belly with the pods that the pigs were eating; and no one gave him anything. Then he came to his senses and said, "How many of my father's paid servants have more food than they can eat, and here am I, starving to death! I will set off and go to my father, and say to him, 'Father, I have sinned, against God and against you; I am no longer fit to be called your son; treat me as one of your paid servants.'" So he set out for his father's house. But while he was still a long way off his father saw him, and his heart went out to him. He ran to meet him, flung his arms round him, and kissed him. The son said, "Father, I have sinned, against God and against you; I am no longer fit to be called your son." But the father said to his servants, "Quick! fetch a robe, my best one, and put it on him; put a ring on his finger and shoes on his feet. Bring the fatted calf and kill it, and let us have a feast to celebrate this day. For this son of mine was dead and has come back to life; he was lost and is found." And the festivities began. Now the elder son was out on the farm; and on his way back, as he approached the house, he heard music and dancing. He called one of the servants and asked what it meant. The servant told him, "Your brother has come home, and your father has killed the fatted calf because he has him back safe and sound." But he was angry and refused to go in. His father came out and pleaded with him; but he retorted, "You know how I have slaved for you all these years; I have never once disobeyed your orders; and you never gave me so much as a kid, for a feast with my friends. But now that this son of yours turns up, after running through your money with his women, you kill the fatted calf for him." "My boy," said the father, "you are always with me, and everything I have is yours. How could we help celebrating this happy day? Your brother here was dead and has come back to life, was lost and is found."

Questions

1 Where did the younger son take his money?

2 What did he do with it?

3 What trouble then came upon the country in which he was living?

4 What would then happen to the price of food?

5 Since the young man was likely to work for wages, why was he starving?

6 How do we know that the father was generous with food in his household?

7 Which sentence suggests that the father had never given up looking for his lost son?

8 How did the father *first* show his excitement at the son's return?

9 The younger son did not complete the speech which he had planned to make to his father. Why was this?

10 When the father sent for the gifts for the son, what message was he giving to the whole household?

11 How did the elder brother first know that a party was being held?

12 When he found out the reason, how did he first show that he was angry?

13 Why did he speak of 'this son of yours' and not of 'my brother'?

14 Why did the elder son think that he had been badly treated?

15 Was he strictly correct in saying that the younger son had spent the *father*'s money ('running through your money')?

16 What did the father mean by saying 'everything I have is yours'? How much land was left for the elder son to inherit?

17 What did the father mean by saying 'Your brother here was dead and has come back to life'?

The meaning of the parable

Jesus left people to work out the message of the story for themselves. Perhaps this is what he hoped they would learn:

1 God is like the father. He loves His children, however stupid or thoughtless they have been, and He will always give them the warm welcome of a generous father.

2 If God is generous and understanding, then His children should be so too. Therefore it was right for Jesus to eat with tax collectors and 'sinners', who were thought to be outcasts.

3 The elder son thought far too much about how well he had done his duty to his father, and his words suggested that he had found it all a great burden. He thought so much about how good he was, that he could not have any kindly feelings for his brother. Instead he *assumed* that the prodigal had spent his money in bad ways.

Strict Jews were blaming Jesus for mixing with sinners. Perhaps they would now ask themselves: 'Are we like the jealous elder brother? Are we assuming that it is more important to perform the heavy duties of our religion than to try to understand the foolish ways of our fellow men and to help them in their troubles?'

A robe for an honoured guest, a ring indicating an official position and a pair of sandals

The great banquet

When Jews thought about the happiness which 'the anointed one' (Messiah) would bring them, they often imagined themselves as taking part in a splendid banquet. This was because meals meant far more to them than simply the taking of food. A Jew would eat only with his friends, and with people whom he respected. He would not eat with a Gentile (non-Jew), or with anybody who was thought to live dishonestly.

Jesus, also, loved the friendliness of meal-times, but he was prepared to eat with anybody, and this shocked many people.

If Luke is right, Jesus told the story of the great banquet when he was eating a meal, on a Sabbath day, in the house of a 'leading Pharisee'.

Pharisees were not priests. They were strict Jews who tried hard in their daily lives to obey all the hundreds of rules which were written in the Jewish books of the Law. They believed sincerely that they would please God most by regular prayer, constant washing, preparing their meals in certain ways, and allowing no work whatever to be done on the Sabbath. They made life very hard for themselves, and they expected other people to copy them, but they also studied the scriptures very carefully to see if there were any hints which might make it easier for them to obey over 600 rules. For example, they read in *Exodus 16 verse 29* 'let no man go out of his place on the seventh day'. If 'his place' meant 'his house', then they must stay indoors all day: but it might have another meaning. They read in *Numbers 35 verse 5* that the pasture land of a city should measure 2000 cubits (about 1000 yards) around the city. They then decided that 'his place' included 2000 cubits in any direction. Therefore they were allowed to make a 'Sabbath day's journey' of up to 2000 cubits.

Yoked oxen in Palestine

The parable Luke 14 verses 16–25

'A man was giving a big dinner party and had sent out many invitations. At dinner-time he sent his servant with a message for his guests, "Please come, everything is now ready." They began one and all to excuse themselves. The first said, "I have bought a piece of land, and I must go and look over it; please accept my apologies." The second said, "I have bought five yoke of oxen, and I am on my way to try them out; please accept my apologies." The next said, "I have just got married and for that reason I cannot come." When the servant came back he reported this to his master. The master of the house was angry and said to him, "Go out quickly into the streets and alleys of the town, and bring me in the poor, the crippled, the blind, and the lame." The servant said, "Sir, your orders have been carried out and there is still room." The master replied, "Go out on to the highways and along the hedgerows and make them come in; I want my house to be full. I tell you that not one of those who were invited shall taste my banquet." '

Questions

1 When did the master of the house send out his servant with the message for the invited guests?

2 Two oxen formed a 'yoke'. Most Jewish farmers needed only one yoke of oxen to work their land. What does this suggest about the guest who needed five yoke?

3 Another guest could afford to buy land, so what does this suggest about the sort of people who were first invited to the banquet?

4 Only men would be invited to a banquet, so the newly-married man would have had to leave his wife at home. Was his excuse any better than the others?

5 Of the guests who were first invited, how many came to the dinner?

6 The poor, the crippled, the blind and the lame were likely all to be beggars. Where was the servant told to find them?

7 Which words of the servant suggest that a large banquet had been planned?

8 What sorts of people would the servant find *a* on the highways? *b* along the hedgerows?

9 What words in the master's last instructions suggest that he expected that some people from the highways and hedgerows would need to be persuaded to come to the house?

An Eastern beggar

The meaning of the parable

It is thought that Jesus was giving this message:

Like the master of the house, I have issued many invitations.

I have invited all people to accept the loving rule of God, and I have told them that the matter is urgent ("everything is now ready").

But it seems that many rich and important people cannot understand what God wants. They are busy with their own affairs, and they think that these are far more worthwhile than my invitation.

The people who will listen to me and accept the rule of God will be those who seem to be completely unimportant—people who seem to have failed in life—people who are despised as well as pitied by successful men and women.

If Jesus was in the house of a leading Pharisee, his host and the other guests may well have felt very uncomfortable after hearing this story. Why?

The labourers in the vineyard

This parable of Jesus is found only in the Gospel of *Matthew 20 verses 1–15*.

'There was once a landowner who went out early one morning to hire labourers for his vineyard; and after agreeing to pay them the usual day's wage he sent them off to work. Going out three hours later he saw some more men standing idle in the market-place. "Go and join the others in the vineyard," he said, "and I will pay you a fair wage"; so off they went. At noon he went out again, and at three in the afternoon, and made the same arrangement as before. An hour before sunset he went out and found another group

standing there; so he said to them, "Why are you
standing about like this all day with nothing to do?"
"Because no one has hired us," they replied; so he
told them, "Go and join the others in the vineyard."
When evening fell, the owner of the vineyard said to
his steward, "Call the labourers and give them their
pay, beginning with those who came last and ending
with the first." Those who had started work an hour
before sunset came forward, and were paid the full
day's wage. When it was the turn of the men who had
come first, they expected something extra, but were
paid the same amount as the others. As they took it,
they grumbled at their employer: "These late-comers
have done only one hour's work, yet you have put
them on a level with us, who have sweated the whole
day long in the blazing sun!" The owner turned to
one of them and said, "My friend, I am not being unfair to you. You agreed on the usual wage for the day,
did you not? Take your pay and go home. I choose to
pay the last man the same as you. Surely I am free to
do what I like with my own money. Why be jealous
because I am kind?" '

A street market in Jerusalem

Notes

1 According to Jewish law, the working day lasted from sunrise until the evening stars appeared.

2 'Early one morning' would be between 6 a.m. and 7 a.m. in our time. The Jews called this 'the first hour'.

3 The 'usual day's wage' was one *denarius*. This was a Roman silver coin. In some Bibles this is translated as 'one penny', but this gives us a quite wrong impression. Four of these coins were enough to buy a lamb, and one denarius was good pay for a day's work.

4 When the grape harvest began, it was important that the grapes should be picked and pressed quickly, before the rainy season came.

Questions

1 When did the employer first go to hire men?

2 What wages did he promise:
  a to the men he hired first?
  b to the men he hired between 9 a.m. and 10 a.m.?

3 How many times altogether did the employer go to hire men?

4 Which sentence suggests that some men could not find other work to do?

A denarius

5 Clearly, the owner did not hire enough men at first. Here are some suggested reasons for this. Which reasons do you think *possible*, and which do you think *unlikely*?

a There were no more men in the market in the early morning.

b The owner did not realize how big the crop of grapes was.

c The owner was short of money.

d Some men in the market did not want to work.

e The owner decided to wait and see how many men he needed.

6 When were the wages paid, and who actually gave them out?

7 Which men were paid first?

8 How much were they paid?

9 What did the first labourers then expect to receive?

10 For how long had these first labourers worked?

11 To whom did they make their complaint?

12 Why did they think that their payment was unfair?

13 What two reasons did the owner give for not agreeing with their complaints?

The meaning of the parable

At the end of the story, Matthew added a verse: 'Thus will the last be first, and the first last.' Clearly, this is what he thought the parable was intended to teach—that people who thought they were the most important were, in fact, the least important. But the last labourers were not paid first in order to show that there was something special about them. They were paid first, in the story, because then the other men would know how much they had been given, and could make their complaint. Matthew must have misunderstood the parable.

We can understand why the grumblers were dissatisfied. They had no legal complaint against the owner, because he had kept his word, but they thought it quite unfair that they should be kept to the strict amount of their bargain while others had been treated so generously.

Therefore Jesus may have been giving this message: 'It would seem very unfair if God, like the employer, gave some men exactly what they deserved, but was very generous to others. But God is not like this. He is generous to *all* men.'

The story can be understood in another way.

The employer paid a full day's wage to the last men because he knew that they could not feed their families on the pay for one hour. In the same way, God is generous, especially to people who are thought to be worthless—people who have done very little.

Jesus may have been saying, to the strict Jews: 'You blame me because I eat with sinners and with other people whom you think worthless. In this way you are like the grumblers in the story, but you have no right to complain. God treats sinners kindly, and I want to do so too, and to make them my friends.'

The good Samaritan

Who is my neighbour? *Luke 10 verses 23–29*

'And behold, a lawyer stood up to put him to the test, saying "Teacher, what shall I do to inherit eternal life?" He said to him, "What is written in the law? How do you read?" And he answered, "You shall love the Lord your God with all your heart, and with all your soul, and with all your strength, and with all your mind; and your neighbour as yourself." And he said to him, "You have answered right; do this, and you will live." But he, desiring to justify himself, said to Jesus, "And who is my neighbour?"'

'A lawyer' means a man who had made a deep study of the laws contained in the Jewish scriptures. It was calculated that 248 of these laws told Jews what they must do, and 365 told them what they must not do. As there was so much to be learnt, some students of the law asked: 'Are there a few basic laws which are so important that all the others can be seen to follow naturally from these few?'

When the lawyer answered the question: 'What is written in the law?' he quoted two verses from the Jewish scriptures, one from *Deuteronomy 6 verse 5* and one from *Leviticus 19 verse 18:*

> 'and you shall love the Lord your God with all your heart, and with all your soul, and with all your might.' (*Deuteronomy*)

> 'You shall not take vengeance or bear any grudge against the sons of your own people, but you shall love your neighbour as yourself.' (*Leviticus*)

Probably these were two verses which other Jews considered to be the most important of all the laws, but it is also possible that Jesus had quoted them as the most important laws in his previous teaching, and that the lawyer knew this. Luke says that he 'stood up to put him to the test', and it may be that the lawyer wanted to trap Jesus into saying: 'If you obey these two, you can forget all the other laws.'

But we cannot be sure of this. It may be that the lawyer was a sincere and troubled man, anxious to know what Jesus thought he ought to do in order to be certain that God would reward him with 'eternal life' after he died.

Jesus told the lawyer that he had given the right answer, and that he would live (that is, have 'eternal life') if he obeyed these two laws in all his actions. However, the lawyer asked another question, because he wanted to 'justify himself'. This may mean that he wanted to show that he was already doing all that he ought to do, or it may mean that he was genuinely puzzled, and wanted Jesus to help him. What did Jesus understand by the word 'neighbour'?

In the verse from Leviticus, 'neighbour' seems to refer to 'the sons of your own people', and it was not hard for a Jew to agree that he ought to show warmth and affection towards his relatives and close friends. But was he obliged to be neighbourly towards Jews who lived in other parts of the country? And, even more important, was it possible for him to think that a Jew who disobeyed the laws was a neighbour? As for Gentiles (people who were not Jews), they, surely did not need to be considered.

Jesus did not give a direct answer. Instead, he told a story, and then asked the lawyer another question.

The parable *Luke 10 verses 30–37*

'Jesus replied, "A man was going down from Jerusalem to Jericho, and he fell among robbers, who stripped him and beat him, and departed, leaving him half-dead. Now by chance a priest was going down

A Jewish priest and a Levite

that road; and when he saw him he passed by on the other side. So likewise a Levite, when he came to the place and saw him, passed by on the other side. But a Samaritan, as he journeyed, came to where he was; and when he saw him, he had compassion, and went to him and bound up his wounds, pouring on oil and wine; then he set him on his own beast and brought him to an inn, and took care of him.

And the next day he took out two denarii and gave them to the inn-keeper, saying, 'Take care of him; and whatever more you spend, I will repay you when I come back.' Which of these three, do you think, proved neighbour to the man who fell among the robbers?" He said, "The one who showed mercy on him." And Jesus said to him, "Go and do likewise." '

Notes

1 Priests were responsible for the daily sacrifices in the Temple, and it was an essential part of their duties that they must avoid anything which might make them 'unclean'. A diseased or a dead body would 'defile' them.

Levites were assistants to the priests, and one of their duties was to slaughter the animals which were sacrificed. It was necessary for them, also, to avoid being 'defiled'.

2 The people who listened to the story would expect that after Jesus had mentioned the priest and the Levite, he would tell of a third person who was an ordinary Jew. Instead, he spoke of a Samaritan, and immediately the feelings of his hearers would turn against this man. Jews and Samaritans hated each other. The northern kingdom of Israel had been conquered by Assyrians in 722 BC, and people from foreign parts had settled in Samaria, the former capital city, and inter-married with the inhabitants. In the centuries which followed, Samaritans claimed that they were worshipping God in the proper way, but the Jews of Judaea denied this, and when they began to rebuild the Temple at Jerusalem after they

returned from Babylonia, they refused to allow the Samaritans to help as they wanted to do. Therefore the Samaritans tried to stop the re-building.

The hatred continued, and Jesus may well have heard of an occasion when Samaritans defiled the Temple by spreading the bones of dead men over one of the courtyards. This was said to have happened between 6 AD and 9 AD, and the first visit of Jesus to Jerusalem was near to this time.

3 Wine would be used as a disinfectant, and oil would soothe the wounds.

4 A denarius was a silver coin (*see page 42*). It is thought that one denarius would have paid for twelve days' lodging at the inn.

5 From Jerusalem to Jericho was a lonely journey of fourteen miles. It still is so.

The old road from Jerusalem to Jericho

Questions

1 Why were robbers likely to attack on the Jerusalem–Jericho road?

2 What did the robbers take from the traveller?

3 Which words tell us that the robbed man was savagely attacked?

4 When the priest and the Levite saw the man lying in the road, what did they probably think?

5 How do we know that they did not make sure that their first impressions were correct?

6 What excuse, if any, could the priest and the Levite have for not helping the wounded man?

7 What was the home country of the next traveller?

8 If the Samaritan did not carry a bandage, how would he be able to bind up the wounds?

9 How do we know that the wounded man was probably unable to walk?

10 For how long could the wounded man stay at the inn for the price of two denarii?

11 The Samaritan expected to travel back past the inn, but not until a number of days had passed. When, probably, did he expect to return?

12 What final question did Jesus ask the lawyer?

13 In his reply, how did the lawyer refer to the Samaritan? What reason might he have for not calling him 'the Samaritan'?

The meaning of the parable

Perhaps the lawyer hoped that Jesus would give him a list of all the sorts of people whom he ought to treat as neighbours. If so,

he was disappointed. Instead, he was told of two men of the
Church who failed to help somebody in great need because they
thought that it was their duty not to risk becoming 'unclean'.
And he was told of a hated foreigner who put all his personal
feelings on one side, saw only a fellow human being in distress,
and took pity on him. Not only did he help him there and then,
but he went out of his way to see that he was cared for until he
was better.

The message is clear. There is no point in making a list of
neighbours. All people are our neighbours, even our enemies.
We must love them all as we love ourselves.

'The Good Samaritan' by Bassano

8 Miracles

We use the word 'miracle' for a remarkable and important happening which nobody can explain. It is different from a trick. If a magician appears to saw a woman in half, we know that we have been deceived, and that he could explain it if he wanted to.

What would be called a miracle at one time may not be thought of as a miracle later. As men learn more about the human body and about the world of nature, there are more and more things which we can explain. We know how men get to the moon, but fifty years ago a man on the moon would have seemed to be the result of a miracle. We know that modern drugs can cure lepers. When Jesus healed lepers he did what nobody could explain, and to the Gospel-writers the healings were a 'wonder', and a 'sign' that Jesus had called upon the power of God.

The Gospel-writers were Jews, and therefore they believed that the world had been created by God. Since God had made the world, it was obvious to them that He could alter it if He wanted to. Therefore they expected that God would sometimes make things happen in ways which nobody could understand. They believed that God had worked miracles through Moses and Elijah and many other heroes of the past, and they were certain

51

The Earth, as it appears from space

that Jesus had been able to ask God to do things which were just as remarkable.

Therefore they expected to hear and read about miracles which Jesus had performed, and, when they found such stories, they accepted them readily though they might decide to make some alterations in the details when they wrote them down. (*See* *p. 5*).

It is because the Gospel-writers *expected* miracles to happen that we should look at their stories very carefully. They may have been only too ready to see a miracle in an event which we might explain in another way.

Questions

1 What things in your own home would appear to perform miracles if they could be seen by a man who died 100 years ago?

2 What often happens to a story which is repeated many times before it is written down?

3 If the details of a story become altered, does this prove that the story was not true when it was first told?

4 Why did the Gospel-writers think that there had been nothing too difficult for Jesus to do?

The miracle-stories in the Gospels are of two main kinds:

1. Miracles of healing
   of mental disorder;
   of bodily disease.
2. Miracles showing control over the forces of nature.

There are also three stories of revival after death. The most remarkable of these is in *John 11 verses 1–46*; but Bible scholars tell us that there are many problems to solve about this story, and that nobody should be required to accept it as an accurate account of what happened.

In reading the other revival stories (*Mark 5 verses 53–54*, and *Luke 7 verses 12–17*) we must remember that doctors no longer call a man dead because he has stopped breathing, or because his heart has stopped beating. Sometimes the breathing or the heartbeat can be started up again.

The daughter of Jairus *Mark 5 verses 21–43*

'As soon as Jesus had returned by boat to the other shore, a great crowd once more gathered round him. While he was by the lakeside, the president of one of the synagogues came up, Jairus by name, and, when he saw him, threw himself down at his feet and pleaded with him. "My little daughter", he said, "is at death's door. I beg you to come and lay your hands on her to cure her and save her life." So Jesus went with him, accompanied by a great crowd which pressed upon him. [*There was an interruption.*] While

[Jesus] was still speaking, a message came from the president's house, "Your daughter is dead; why trouble the Rabbi further?" But Jesus, overhearing the message as it was delivered, said to the president of the synagogue, "Do not be afraid; only have faith." After this he allowed no one to accompany him except Peter and James and James's brother John. They came to the president's house, where he found a great commotion, with loud crying and wailing. So he went in and said to them, "Why this crying and commotion? The child is not dead: she is asleep." But they only laughed at him. After turning all the others out, he took the child's father and mother and his own companions and went in where the child was lying. Then, taking hold of her hand, he said to her, "*Talitha cum,*" which means, "Get up, my child." Immediately the girl got up and walked about—she was twelve years old. And they were overcome with amazement. He gave them strict orders to let no one hear about it, and told them to give her something to eat.'

Matthew 9 verses 18–26 gives a shortened version of the story but says that the child was already dead before her father came to Jesus, and that flute-players had been called into the house to assist in the mourning.

Luke 8 verses 40–56 says that the child was the *only* daughter of Jairus.

Questions

1 *Talitha cum* are Aramaic words and Mark thought it necessary to translate them for his readers. What does this tell us about the people for whom Mark was writing?

2 Which Gospel does not tell us the daughter's age?

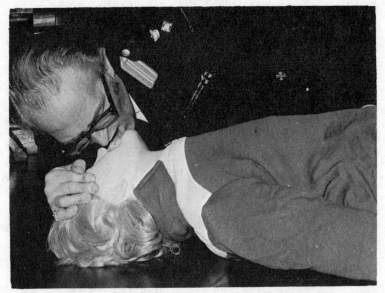

The 'kiss of life' method of artificial respiration can sometimes be used to restart a person's breathing

3 According to Mark and Luke, who first decided that the child was dead?

4 Mark, Matthew and Luke told this as the story of a miracle. Is any other explanation possible?

The healing miracles

The Jews believed that if a man was ill, he was being punished by God for his sins. They also believed that devils could enter into people and cause them to have fits or to become mad. This was their explanation of what we call mental illness.

Jesus told his disciples that disease was not a punishment for sin: 'As he went on his way Jesus saw a man blind from his birth. His disciples put the question, "Rabbi, who sinned, this man or his parents? Why was he born blind?" "It is not that this man or his parents sinned," Jesus answered.' (*John 9 verse 3*).

On several occasions Jesus healed people whose minds were seriously disturbed, and, according to the Gospel-writers, he spoke as if the trouble was caused by evil spirits. For example, the first cure recorded by Mark is described as follows: 'They came to Capernaum, and on the Sabbath he went to the synagogue and began to teach. The people were astounded at his teaching, for, unlike the doctors of the law, he taught with a note of authority. Now there was a man in the synagogue possessed by an unclean spirit. He shrieked: "What do you want with us, Jesus of Nazareth? Have you come to destroy us? I know who you are—the Holy One of God." '

Note

When people said that Jesus taught or spoke 'with authority', they meant that his words were completely clear, and that he expected people to do what he said.

> 'Jesus rebuked him: "Be silent," he said, "and come out of him." And the unclean spirit threw the man into convulsions and with a loud cry left him. They were all amazed and began to ask one another, "What is this? A new kind of teaching! He speaks with authority. When he gives orders, even the unclean spirits submit." The news spread rapidly, and he was spoken of all over the district of Galilee.' (*Mark 1 verses 21–28*)

The leaders of the Jewish Religion heard that Jesus was healing sick people, and that his teaching was thought to be much more impressive than that of the normal preachers—'doctors of the law', who had made a special study of the Jewish scriptures. The leaders were disturbed and angry. They thought that Jesus must be stopped before he had done too much damage, and they tried to prove that he was using what we would call 'black magic'. The Jews believed that there was a Prince of Devils called Beelzebub, and that some people could call on him to control evil spirits.

What happened is described in *Mark 3 verses 20–24:*

'[Jesus] entered a house; and once more such a crowd collected round them that they had no chance to eat. When his family heard of this, they set out to take charge of him; for people were saying that he was out of his mind.

The doctors of the law, too, who had come down from Jerusalem said, "He is possessed by Beelzebub," and, "He drives out devils by the prince of devils." So he called them to come forward, and spoke to them in parables: "How can Satan drive out Satan?" '

By this Jesus probably meant: 'If I am working for Satan [Beelzebub] and the evil spirits are also working for him, is it likely that Satan would use me to drive out his own workers?'

Does this show that Jesus really believed that mental illness was caused by evil spirits? We cannot tell, since Jesus spoke in words and ideas which his hearers would understand. His own thoughts may have been quite different.

The doctors of the law, who were opposed to Jesus, did not say that the healings had not occurred, or that they had been faked in some way. Instead, they accused him of using black magic: and this is very important. It means that they knew that Jesus really had been healing the sick. They had to admit it because of what they had heard from the people of Galilee. (If the friend of a man says that he has done a kind action, we may think that he says it merely because he is a friend. If the enemy of a man says that he has done a kind action, we are much more likely to accept it as true).

Questions

1 What evidence suggests that Jesus' own family did not understand him?

2 Give two names for the Prince of Devils.

3 What did Jesus mean by the question: 'How can Satan drive out Satan?'

4 How do the 'doctors of the law' from Jerusalem help to convince us that Jesus healed the sick?

Many stories tell us that Jesus cured diseases of the body. These included fever (*Mark 1 verses 21–28*), leprosy (*Mark 1 verses 40–45, Luke 17 verses 12–10*), epilepsy (*Mark 9 verses 14–29*), lameness, paralysis, and a bent body (*Mark 2 verses 1–12, Matthew 8 verses 5–13, Luke 7 verses 1–10, John 5 verses 1–18, Luke 13 verses 10–17*), dropsy (painful swellings) (*Luke 14 verses 1–6*), a withered hand (*Mark 3 verses 1–6*) and continued bleeding (*Mark 5 verses 25–34*). There were also several healings of people who were blind or dumb, or both blind and dumb (*Mark 8 verses 22–26, Mark 10 verses 46–52, Matthew 9 verses 27–31, Matthew 12 verse 22, John 9 verses 1–34*).

If we read these stories one after another, certain things become very clear:

a Jesus cured people because he was sorry for them. In Matthew 20 verse 34 'Jesus was deeply moved, and touched their eyes.'

A pacemaker, which is used for certain heart conditions. The wire leads to a device implanted in the body

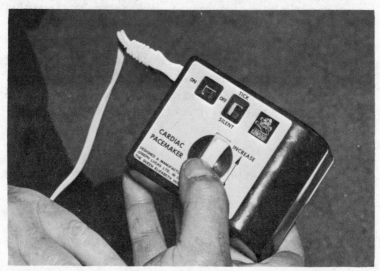

b Jesus was most anxious not to be talked about as just somebody who could work wonders. Often we are told that he ordered the cured people not to say who had helped them, but it seems strange that he thought they would be able to keep quiet about it.

c Many people (as well as the 'doctors') accused Jesus of using black magic.

d Many of the healings took place on the Sabbath day. This was a shocking scandal to strict Jews (*see page 93*).

e On some occasions we are told that Jesus emphasized that the cure occurred *only* because the sick person *knew* that it could happen—that is, because he had *faith* in Jesus.

Matthew tells us that Jesus said to two blind men, 'Do you believe that I have the power to do what you want?' 'Yes, sir,' they said. Then he touched their eyes, and said, 'As you have believed, so let it be'; and their sight was restored. Jesus said to them sternly, 'See that no one hears about this.' But as soon as they had gone out they talked about him all over the countryside. (*Matthew 9 verses 28–31*)

In a similar way, Jesus told a leper 'your faith has cured you' (*Luke 17 verse 19*).

The faith that Jesus looked for was not a vague belief in the goodness of God. It was the simple and complete certainty in the mind of the sick man that God had the power to help him, when all human help had failed; and that Jesus could call upon the power of God.

Mark tells of an occasion when Jesus went back among the people who had known him as a boy. They were impressed by his teaching, but somehow they could not take him seriously.

'Jesus said to them, "A prophet will always be held in honour except in his home town, and among his kinsmen and family." He could work no miracle there, except that he put his hands on a few sick people and healed them; and he was taken aback by their want of faith.' (*Mark 6 verses 1–6*)

No Gospel-writer would wish to tell of an apparent failure by Jesus. This story, therefore, is almost certainly true, and it underlines the suggestion that Jesus needed the sick people to have faith in him.

We still know very little about the ways in which our bodily health can be affected by the ways in which we feel and think. Many people today are cured of disease even though their doctors have not been able to find a complete remedy. Some of these people are certain that they have been cured by faith.

The miracles of control over nature

The Gospel-writers were convinced that Jesus was the Son of God, and therefore it was obvious to them that he could control the forces of nature as he wished. They described how:

1 He gave orders to the winds and the waves. (*Mark 4 verses 35–44*)

2 He guided Peter, who had caught no fish, to a part of the lake where he had an enormous haul. (*Luke 5 verses 1–11*)

3 He knew that a certain fish would have a valuable coin in its mouth. (*Matthew 17 verses 24–27*)

4 He caused a fig tree to wither because it had no fruit when he wanted it. (*Mark 11 verses 12–14, 20–25*)

5 He turned water into wine. (*John 2 verses 1–11*)

6 He walked on water. (*Mark 6 verses 45–52: John 6 verses 16–21*)

7 He fed great crowds of people with a few loaves and fishes. (*Mark 6 verses 30–44, Mark 8 verses 1–10*)

Bible scholars have studied these stories with the greatest possible care, and have decided that they cannot be certain that any one of them gives a completely accurate picture of what happened. For example, Mark wrote that during a storm Jesus 'said to the sea, "Hush! Be still!" '. But perhaps Jesus was really speaking to the disciples, who were agitated and were moving about the boat in a panic.

The Sea of Galilee

Another story reads:

> 'At nightfall his disciples went down to the sea, got into their boat, and pushed off to cross the water to Capernaum. Darkness had already fallen, and Jesus had not yet joined them. By now a strong wind was blowing and the sea grew rough. When they had rowed about three or four miles they saw Jesus walking on the sea and approaching the boat. They were terrified, but he called out, "It is I; do not be afraid." Then they were ready to take him aboard, and immediately the boat reached the land they were making for.' (*John 6 verses 16–21*)

One important point here is that the Greek words translated 'walking on the water' would normally mean 'walking *by* the water'. But why, then, should the disciples be terrified at seeing Jesus? One suggestion is that when the story was first told it was about an event which happened *after* the Crucifixion. This would certainly explain why the disciples thought Jesus was a ghost, as Mark says that they did. (*Mark 6 verse 49*)

We must be careful not to misunderstand what the Bible scholars tell us. They do *not* say that Jesus was unable to per-

form miracles. What they do say is that the Gospel-writers may
have altered some of the miracle stories in order to drive home
certain lessons which they wished to impress upon the people for
whom the Gospels were written (and they were not written for
us). These lessons were:
1 That God, acting through Jesus, had given help when
everybody else had failed.
2 That in order to receive this help, a Christian must have faith.
That is, he must believe whole-heartedly that the help would be
given.

So, for the Gospel-writers, the lessons were more important
than the details of the stories which they heard or read.
Therefore they thought it right to alter certain details in order to
make the lessons as clear as possible.

For this reason, it is often impossible for us to know just
how the stories ran when they were first told and repeated—that
is, at the time when they first became part of the 'tradition' of the
Christian Church. (*See page 4.*)

Mark 6, verses 32–44

'[Jesus and the disciples] set off privately by boat for
a lonely place. But many saw them leave and
recognized them, and came round by land, hurrying
from all the towns towards the place, and arrived
there first. When he came ashore, he saw a great
crowd; and his heart went out to them, because they
were like sheep without a shepherd; and he had much
to teach them. As the day wore on, his disciples approached him and said, "This is a lonely place and it
is getting very late; send the people off to the farms
and villages round about, to buy themselves
something to eat." "Give them something to eat
yourselves," he answered. They replied, "Are we to
go and spend twenty pounds on bread to give them a
meal?" "How many loaves have you?" he asked; "go
and see." They found out and told him, "Five, and

two fishes also." He ordered them to make the people sit down in groups on the green grass, and they sat down in rows, a hundred rows of fifty each. Then, taking the five loaves and the two fishes, he looked up to heaven, said the blessing, broke the loaves and gave them to the disciples to distribute. He also divided the two fishes among them. They all ate to their hearts' content; and twelve great basketfuls of scraps were picked up, with what was left of the fish. Those who ate the loaves numbered five thousand men.'

Mark 8, verses 1–9

'There was another occasion about this time when a huge crowd had collected, and, as they had no food, Jesus called his disciples and said to them, "I feel sorry for all these people; they have been with me now for three days and have nothing to eat. If I send them home unfed, they will turn faint on the way; some of them have come from a distance." The disciples answered, "How can anyone provide all these people with bread in this lonely place?" "How many loaves have you?" he asked; and they answered, "Seven." So he ordered the people to sit down on the ground; then he took the seven loaves, and, after giving thanks to God, he broke the bread and gave it to his disciples to distribute; and they served it out to the people. They had also a few small fishes, which he blessed and ordered them to distribute. They all ate to their hearts' content, and seven baskets were filled with the scraps that were left. The people numbered about four thousand.'

(The best-known version of the first story is given by *John 6 verses 1–13*. Somewhat different accounts appear in *Matthew 14 verses 13–21*, and *Luke 9 verses 10–17*. The second story is told in *Matthew 15 verses 29–39* as well as by Mark.)

Questions on these two stories

Draw two columns in your notebook and head one Mark 6 and the other Mark 8. Then answer the following questions:

1   In what sort of place was Jesus teaching?

2   For how long were the people there?

3   Who first thought about the need for food?

4   Whose loaves were used?

5   How many loaves?

6   How many fishes?

7   What did Jesus do before he broke the bread?

8   Who gave out the food?

9   How many baskets of scraps were collected?

10   How many people were present?

Pilgrims at Lourdes, in France, where miracles are said to have occurred

We are bound to ask: did two very similar incidents occur, or did Mark and Matthew both write down two different accounts of the same event?

Perhaps the most important clue is in Mark 8 verse 4, when the disciples asked Jesus: 'How can anyone provide all these people with bread in this lonely place?'

If there were two separate incidents, it seems impossible that the disciples had forgotten what Jesus had done on the first occasion. Yet they asked a question which suggested that they had no idea at all of what Jesus might do.

Most scholars now think that the six accounts in the Gospels all describe the same incident. But what really happened?

It is impossible to be certain, especially as no account says that Jesus actually *multiplied* the loaves and fishes. All we can say is that the Gospel-writers had heard of an occasion when Jesus ate with a large crowd of people, and when, because of his help, they had all been completely satisfied, although there had seemed to be very little food.

Perhaps, also, we can learn something from the report that no litter was left on the grass.

Conclusions

The Gospel-writers thought that the miracle-stories would help to convince people that Jesus was the Son of God.

Jesus said that it was God who performed the miracles, and he never tried to use his healings in order to impress people and to prove how important he was.

It follows that we should not be asked to argue that the miracle stories *prove* that Jesus was the Son of God. But they do show us that Jesus was always deeply concerned about people in trouble.

As we read the Gospels, it is only sensible for us to remember that some of the stories may have been altered and exaggerated, and that some may have been misunderstood. But it is not sensible to say: 'We have never seen a miracle: therefore miracles never have happened, and never will happen.'

9 Living under the rule of God

Love your neighbour as yourself

The Jews believed that God was merciful and ready to forgive, but they thought that His main interest was in men who obeyed His laws, and that He would give no help to sinners until they had repented and changed their whole way of living.

Jesus challenged these thoughts by saying that God had a special love for sinners, and that people must trust him to know that this was true. Then, if they thought of God and talked to God as he told them to do, they would begin to know the great joy of living under the Rule of God.

They must make their decision at once. But if they accepted the challenge, how would God require them to live?

Jesus said that any man who lived as a child of God would want to do nothing but good to his fellow men, and because he *wanted* this he would find out how to do it. Detailed rules were not needed, and so there is no list, based on the words of Jesus, to tell men how to behave in all their daily actions. There is nothing like the 613 regulations which the Pharisees tried to obey.

Jesus said that the two most important rules of the Jewish scriptures were:

'Love the Lord your God with all your heart, with all
your mind, and with all your srength.
Love your neighbour as yourself.'

Then he gave new meaning to both sentences by saying that
God must be loved as a child loves his father; and that a man
who lives as a child of God will think even of his enemies as his
neighbours. (*see page 45*.)

He also said that a man's thoughts and feelings were just as
important as his actions. To hate a man enough to want to kill
him was at least as evil as actually committing murder.

'You have learned that our forefathers were told, "Do
not commit murder; anyone who commits murder
must be brought to judgement." But what I tell you is
this; anyone who nurses anger against his brother
must be brought to judgement.' (*Matthew 5 verses
21–22*)

These verses come from the part of the Gospel which is
usually called the Sermon on the Mount, because Matthew
writes: 'When he saw the crowds he went up the hill. There he
took his seat, and when his disciples had gathered round him he
began to address them.'

A hill near the Sea of Galilee

Luke (*chapter 6*) gives many of the same sayings of Jesus, but pictures him talking to his disciples on level ground among a large crowd of people.

It seems certain that both Matthew and Luke put together teachings which Jesus gave on a number of different occasions, and that both were using a collection of sayings of the sort which was mentioned on page 3.

It has been thought that Luke kept more closely than Matthew to the words which he was copying. Jesus was giving examples of how men would live if they were under the rule of God.

Luke, chapter 6

28 'Love your enemies; do good to those who hate you; bless those who curse you; pray for those who treat
29 you spitefully. When a man hits you on the cheek, offer him the other cheek too; when a man takes your
30 coat, let him have your shirt as well. Give to everyone who asks you; when a man takes what is yours, do
31 not demand it back. Treat others as you would like them to treat you.'

Notes

1 Verse 28. How is it possible to love our personal enemies, people who hate us? Jesus said: do them a good turn and pray for them. This may seem unnatural, but hatred can be cured only by positive actions.

2 Verse 29. Matthew's words are: 'If someone slaps you on the right cheek, turn and offer him your left.'

Imagine yourself facing a man who slaps you with his right hand. Which part of his hand will hit your right cheek? The Jews regarded a back-handed slap as a great insult.

3 Verse 29. In a very hot climate a man would be unlikely to wear much more than a coat and a shirt; therefore, if he allowed a thief to take both, he would be practically naked.

4 Verse 29. Matthew's words are: 'If a man wants to sue you for your shirt, let him have your coat as well.'

A Jewish coat and shirt

This means that Matthew thought that Jesus was speaking about a man **A** who claimed in a law court that another man **B** had taken his shirt. According to Jewish law, the court would assume that the shirt belonged to **B**, and **A** would not be able to have it back unless he could *prove* that it belonged to him; and this might be difficult.

Matthew thought that Jesus was saying: 'Be generous, even in a court of law. If you have something which belongs to another man, let him have it even if he cannot prove that it is his, and give him something else as well.'

5 Verse 30. The second part is difficult to understand. One suggestion is that Jesus meant: 'When you have lent a men something which he needs, let him keep it as long as he wants. Stop worrying him to let you have it back.'

6 Verse 31. The Jews had a saying: 'What thou hatest, do to no man.' Jesus went beyond this and said: 'Think what kindnesses you would like other people to do for you, and be kind to them in the same way.' This is often called the Golden Rule.

Questions

1 According to the Jews, what must sinners do before God would be ready to help them?

2 According to Jesus, what did God feel about sinners?

3 According to Jesus, why should a man not need detailed rules about how to do good to his fellow men?

4 Why are a man's thoughts and feelings just as important as his actions?

5 Luke, chapter 6 is often called the Sermon on the Plain. Why is this?

6 Jesus gave striking examples of how people living under the rule of God would behave, but verse 29 (second part) can hardly have been intended as an exact instruction. Why not?

Love your enemies

Luke, chapter 6

32 'If you love only those who love you, what credit is that to you? Even sinners love those who love them.

33 Again, if you do good only to those who do good to you, what credit is that to you? Even sinners do as

34 much. And if you lend only where you expect to be repaid, what credit is that to you? Even sinners lend

35 to each other if they are to be repaid in full. But you must love your enemies and do good; and lend without expecting any return; and you will have a rich reward: you will be sons of the Most High, because he himself is kind to the ungrateful and

36 wicked. Be compassionate as your Father is com-

37 passionate. Pass no judgement, and you will not be judged; do not condemn, and you will not be condemned.'

Notes

1 Verses 32–34. When Jews spoke of 'sinners' they meant:
a Gentiles (non-Jews), who did not know the Jewish Law.
b Jews who knew the Law but failed to keep to its rules.

Jesus is saying that to help one's friends is a matter of common sense and decency which anybody can understand. But living under the rule of God means going far beyond this.

2 Verse 35. 'Most High' is a name for God which is one translation of the Hebrew name *El Elyon* which means 'Highest God'.

3 Verse 36. 'Compassionate' means 'Able to feel and share the sufferings of other people, understanding their troubles, and so helping to make them more bearable'.

4 Verse 37. When a man does something which seems to be evil, we may say that what he does is wrong (as we see it), but we may not say that he is an evil man. God, alone, is able to know why a man behaves as he does: no human being can know all the facts. We must always give our fellow men the 'benefit of the doubt', assuming that they acted from good motives and not from bad. We may not 'pass judgement' upon the people we know unless we are willing to accept judgement according to a similar standard (see Matthew 7 verses 1–2).

In all his teaching, Jesus took what was best in the Jewish religion and explained that it must be carried much further. He said:

> 'Do not suppose that I have come to abolish the Law and the prophets; I did not come to abolish, but to complete,' (*Matthew 5, verse 17*)

The Jewish Law had tried to state the will of God. Scribes and Pharisees had struggled, sincerely, to carry out the Law in all its detail, but they had bothered so much about the daily regulations that they had failed to think much about the needs of their fellow men. In this sense their very religion made them put heavy burdens upon their neighbours, because they thought that all Jews ought to try to carry out the daily rules.

Jesus said that some rules were useful, but that for a child of God, love must come first. Everything else would follow, and rules would be put in their proper place.

Jesus said that for any man who really knew that he was a child of God it would be *natural* to live as God wanted, because this would be what he, also, wanted above everything else. He would be supremely happy, however hard his life, but he would not be obeying God in order to obtain a reward. By loving his fellow men he would be simply showing his true nature.

Were these teachings of Jesus intended only for his disciples? Did they describe an ideal society, with standards which were far too difficult for ordinary men to achieve? Did Jesus expect that Jews, under the control of a Roman army, would really be able to love their enemies; or was he thinking only of private enemies, in a man's own town?

It is not surprising that these questions have been discussed, time and again, throughout the centuries. But the basic message of the Gospels is clear. To live under the rule of God, a man must *want* to go far beyond all the standards of good behaviour and kindliness which normal people accept as reasonable and possible.

Questions

1 What did the Jews mean by 'sinners'?

2 Name two groups of people whom the Jews would regard as enemies.

3 What is the meaning of 'Most High'? (verse 35)

4 Give an example of a 'compassionate' action. (verse 36)

5 Why may one man not 'condemn' another? (verse 37)

6 In what words did Jesus make it plain that he had no wish to do away with the Jewish Law?

7 How had the Pharisees put heavy burdens upon their neighbours?

8 Which of these statements gives the best summary of the teaching of Jesus?

a Love your neighbour, in order to obtain God's reward.

b Love your enemy, because then he will treat you well.

c Accept the rule of God, and then you will want to love your enemies, who are also children of God.

d Be kind to your neighbour, because you never know when you may want his help.

A Pharisee

10 What did Jesus say about himself?

Did Jesus say that he was the Son of God, meaning that he was divine as well as human?

Did Jesus claim to be the Messiah? This is a different question, because the Jews thought of the Messiah as a great leader sent by God, but they did not think of him as divine.

The questions are not easy to answer, because we know the words of Jesus *only* through the Gospels, and John alone states quite certainly that Jesus claimed to be the Son of God.

In the Gospels of Matthew, Mark and Luke:

a Jesus does not claim to be the Son of God.

b There is no clear proof that he wanted to be called 'Messiah', even in private.

Jewish names for the Messiah were 'Son of David' and 'Son of Man'. Jesus said that he came from the family of David, but he did not call himself 'Son of David'. This title would have suggested wars and conquests.

In all four Gospels it is only once reported that Jesus, without being asked, claimed that he was the Messiah. The story is told by John (*4, verses 7–26*). Jesus was speaking privately to a Samaritan woman who had come to draw water from a well, and after some talk about the religion of the Samaritans:

74

'The woman answered, "I know that Messiah ... is coming. When he comes he will tell us everything." Jesus said, "I am he, I who am speaking to you now." '

John also writes that on a winter's day in Jerusalem, the crowds asked Jesus: 'How long must you keep us in suspense? If you are the Messiah say so plainly.' 'I have told you,' said Jesus, 'but you do not believe.'

Matthew, Mark and Luke all report a conversation with the disciples. This is Mark's account (*Mark 8, verses 27–33*)

'Jesus and his disciples set out for the villages of Caesarea Philippi. On the way he asked his disciples, "Who do men say that I am?" They answered, "Some say John the Baptist, others Elijah, others one of the prophets." "And you," he asked, "who do you say that I am?" Peter replied: "You are the Messiah." Then he gave them strict orders not to tell anyone about him; and he began to teach them that the Son of Man had to undergo great sufferings, and to be rejected by the elders, chief priests, and doctors of the law ... At this Peter took him by the arm and began to rebuke him. But Jesus turned round, and, looking at his disciples, rebuked Peter, "Away with you, Satan," he said; "you think as men think, not as God thinks."'

Thus, Jesus did not refuse the title of Messiah, but he told the disciples that the Son of Man would be made to suffer greatly. Peter assumed that Jesus was talking about the Messiah, and was shocked, because Jews expected the Messiah to lead them to glory, not to suffering and disgrace. Peter therefore told Jesus that he was wrong, and Jesus rebuked Peter for thinking that the Messiah might be able to avoid a painful death. It was men, and not God, who thought of the Messiah in this way.

Matthew, Mark and Luke tell us that on one other vital occasion, when he was questioned by the High Priest, Jesus was asked the double question: 'Are you the Messiah? Are you the Son of God?' (*see page 90*).

These are the recorded answers:

> Luke: 'If I tell you, you will not believe me.'
> (*22, verse 67*)
>
> Matthew: 'The words are yours' (or, 'You have said so.')
> (*26, verse 64*).
>
> Mark: 'I am.'
> (*14, verse 62*).

Some scholars think that Mark has not copied the reply which was given in the story he was using, but when we put the three answers together, we can safely conclude that Jesus did not say: 'I am **not** the Messiah.' Yet this reply might have saved his life.

The crowd picked up stones on more than one occasion

If Jesus was prepared to face death rather than deny that he was the Messiah, why would he not accept the title openly?

Two reasons have been suggested:

1 Jesus wanted people to trust him because of his whole way of living and talking, and not because he had a majestic title. (Just as a good general may try to win the confidence of his men because of the way in which he leads them, and not because of his rank.)

2 Jesus knew that if he called himself Messiah, Jews would expect him to be the sort of leader they had hoped for. This would cause only confusion and misunderstanding, because Jesus knew, almost certainly, that he would be condemned to death, and it was impossible for the Jews to imagine that this could happen to the Messiah.

Jesus may not have foreseen that he would be crucified, but he knew that he might be stoned. He had 'worked' on the Sabbath Day, and he had said things about God which many Jews thought wicked. Before the Roman occupation, both these offences had been punished by stoning, and, according to John (*10, verse 31*) the crowds picked up stones on more than one occasion.

In the extract on page 75 Jesus said that the 'Son of Man' had to undergo great sufferings. When this name was first used (in Aramaic) it meant simply 'Man' or 'Mankind'. Later, the Jews used the name for the Messiah, because they had read in the Book of Daniel 7, verse 13:

> 'I saw in the night visions, and behold, with the clouds of heaven there came one like a son of man.'

Jesus often spoke about the Son of Man, and the Gospel-writers assumed that he was talking about himself. Yet he always spoke of him as another person: he never said, 'I am the Son of Man'. For this reason there is still some doubt about what Jesus meant when he used the name.

In 1492, Columbus landed in the West Indies, but thought that he was in China. He never *claimed* to be the discoverer of the West Indies, but he was so, none the less.

It is important to realize that in this section we have been concerned only with the question: 'Did Jesus *claim* to be the Messiah and the Son of God?'

Jesus may have had very good reasons for not wanting to make this claim, and even if we decided that he did *not* make it, we are still left with a much more important question: '*Was* Jesus the Messiah and the Son of God?'

Questions

1 Which Gospel-writer was certain that Jesus claimed to be the Son of God?

2 Which name for 'Messiah' did Jesus certainly not use?

3 Why did the title 'Son of David' suggest wars and conquests? (see page 74).

4 In which Gospel is it reported that Jesus, without being asked, said that he was the Messiah?

5 To whom did Jesus say this?

6 How did Jesus shock Peter?

7 Why did Jesus rebuke Peter?

8 When the High Priest put his question to Jesus, what can we safely say about the answer?

9 In the Aramaic language, what was the original meaning of the name which is translated 'Son of Man'?

10 Why can we not be certain that Jesus spoke of himself as 'Son of Man'?

11 The Lord's Prayer

Luke 11, verses 1–4

'He was praying in a certain place, and when he ceased, one of his disciples said to him, "Lord, teach us to pray, as John taught his disciples." And he said to them, "When you pray say:

Father, hallowed be thy name. Thy kingdom come. Give us each day our daily bread; and forgive us our sins, for we ourselves forgive everyone who is indebted to us; and lead us not into temptation."'

Matthew 6, verses 5–13

'And when you pray, you must not be like the hypocrites; for they love to stand and pray in the synagogues and at the street corners, that they may be seen by men. Truly, I say to you, they have their reward. But when you pray, go into your room and shut the door and pray to your Father who is in secret; and your Father who sees in secret will reward you.

And in praying do not heap up empty phrases as the Gentiles do; for they think that they will be heard

79

for their many words. Do not be like them, for your Father knows what you need before you ask him. Pray then like this:

> Our Father who art in heaven,
> Hallowed be thy name.
> Thy kingdom come,
> Thy will be done,
>   On earth as it is in heaven.
> Give us this day our daily bread;
> And forgive us our debts,
>   As we also have forgiven our debtors;
> And lead us not into temptation,
> But deliver us from evil.'

(The remaining verses normally recited, which begin: 'For thine is the kingdom . . .' were not part of the original prayer. They were added by the Early Christian Church.)

Jews praying at the Wailing Wall in Jerusalem

The original prayer

It is assumed that there was only one occasion when Jesus taught this prayer to the disciples, and therefore we have to ask why Matthew's version is longer than Luke's.

After a very detailed study of the Greek in which the passages were written, Bible scholars have decided that Jesus probably gave a prayer as short as that in Luke, and that Matthew added certain sentences in order to make the meaning more clear. They have also decided that where the two versions are almost the same, the wording given by Matthew is probably more accurate than that given by Luke.

If these suggestions are accepted, the best English translation of the words of Jesus seems to be:

Father,

Hallowed be thy name;

Thy kingdom come.

Give us this day our daily bread:

and forgive us our debts, as we also have forgiven our debtors.

And lead us not into temptation.

Questions

1 Who was the John referred to by the disciples in the extract from Luke?

2 Who were 'hypocrites', and what was wrong with the way in which they prayed?

3 In Matthew's version of the prayer, which sentences are not found in any form in the prayer as given by Luke?

The Lord's Prayer is the best known of all those used by the Christian Church, and it can be taken as a summary of what Jesus taught about prayer. Scholars have searched for the meaning of each word and sentence, and have then shown that much can be learnt also from the order in which the sentences were spoken. The most important prayers come first.

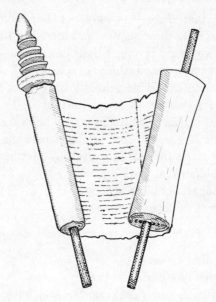

A Jewish prayer roll

Father

Jesus tells the disciples that they can forget the elaborate opening words which were addressed to God in many Jewish prayers. They may speak to God simply as 'Father', and remember that they are His children.

Hallowed be thy name; Thy kingdom come

Jews thought that a man's name was something extremely important. It was not just a label, which enabled him to be recognized. It was very much a part of him, and he might be gravely offended if somebody insulted his name. (It was for this reason that Jews tried hard not to mention the name of God directly. Instead, they spoke of 'the Lord', or 'the Blessed'.)

A man's name could stand for:
the man himself;
the man's actions;
everything that the man intended to do.

So, the name of God can stand for all the things which God wants his people to do. To 'hallow' means 'to treat with reverence', and the name of God is hallowed when people act as God wishes them to do, and so do their utmost to carry out God's plans for the world. The disciples are told to pray that this may happen.

'Thy kingdom come" is a similar prayer. We have seen on page 28 that Jesus spoke of the rule or reign of God as the 'kingdom' of God. The words have the same meaning here. Jesus is telling his disciples that they should pray, first of all, that the rule of God may be established quickly, because they want to be able to help God to defeat the evil in the world. They want his 'kingdom' urgently, and they pray for other people to want it.

Give us this day our daily bread

This has often been understood to mean: 'I pray for plain food, and the other bare necessities of life', but many scholars think that this is too simple an explanation. They point out that the Greek word which has been translated 'daily' is a most unusual word, and that the true meaning may be: 'Give us this day our bread for the morrow', that is the 'bread' which we will need in the future.

According to the Gospel of John, when Jesus spoke of bread he was often thinking of the special help which people would need in order to make it possible for them to live under the rule of God. He meant the 'bread of life', which would feed their spirit, not baker's bread which would feed their body.

If this is the true meaning of 'daily bread', then the whole of the prayer up to this point asks: 'May the rule of God come quickly, and may we be given the strength to play our part in this kingdom.'

The disciples had often heard Jewish prayers which asked God to defeat the evil in the world and to set up his promised kingdom. But these were elaborate and lengthy prayers which thought of the Messiah as a national leader, who would bring the scattered Jews under his rule, and free them from the Roman governors. The prayer of Jesus is simple and short, and makes no reference to any struggle for freedom against Rome.

And forgive us our debts, as we also have forgiven our debtors

By 'debts' the disciples would understand 'sins'. Jesus had often told them that God would forgive their sins, that is, that he would feel towards them and act towards them as if the wrongs had never been done. But this part of the prayer makes it plain that a man cannot be forgiven unless he is ready to forgive all the people who have done wrong to him. The wording of the prayer seems to suggest that a man should ask God to forgive him because he has *already* forgiven other people, but some scholars think that the best translation of the sentence is: 'And forgive us our debts, as we also *will forgive* our debtors'.

Whichever is the correct translation, the sentence means that the men who receive God's forgiveness are those who are sympathetic and forgiving towards other people. It is they who know what forgiveness means, and so they are able to receive the forgiveness of God.

And lead us not into temptation

'Temptation', here, means a time of severe testing. Jews believed that, in the end, God would defeat all the powers of evil in the world, but that when the final struggle came, it would bring terrible suffering for men and women.

Jesus had taught the disciples to ask that the rule of God may come quickly. Now he told them to pray that they might be strong enough to play their full part in the troubled times ahead. They were to pray that they might have the courage to endure every trial or temptation which they might be called upon to face.

The order of the prayers

Jesus says:

> 'Ask first, for the coming of the rule of God;
> then, for your basic needs (or for "spiritual" food);
> then, for forgiveness;
> then, for strength.'

So, Jesus teaches that prayer is a talk with God, the Father of all, and that the man who prays should wish, with all his heart and mind, that the rule of God may be established in the world. Then he can expect his prayers to be answered. It is of such people that Jesus says: 'Ask, and it will be given you.' (*Luke 11, verse 9*)

Questions

1 What was the Aramaic word which Jesus used for God (see page 28)?

2 How does the wording of Luke's prayer show that Jews spoke of sins as debts?

3 What is the meaning of 'forgive'?

4 In which parable had Jesus taught that God was always ready to forgive sinners?

5 In which account of a period in the life of Jesus was the word 'temptation' used to mean a severe testing or trial?

12 Why was Jesus condemned to death?

Mark, Luke, Matthew and John all told how Jesus was condemned to death, but they were not writing so that we could study the story in the twentieth century. They were writing for the people of their own time, in particular for the Jews, who had to be persuaded that their Messiah had already come; and for the Romans (and other Gentiles) who were often more ready than the Jews to hear about Jesus.

For the Jews, the great stumbling block was that Jesus had been punished as if he were an enemy of God and a criminal. When the Jews read passages in their Scriptures which seemed to be about the Messiah, how could they possibly think that God would have allowed him to suffer in this way?

The Gospel-writers tried to show that if these passages were understood properly, they foretold what had happened to Jesus. They tried to prove that at every step, Jesus had acted in the way that God had planned for him.

The Romans' main objection was that Christians asked them to follow the teachings of a man who had been executed as a traitor to the state. Therefore it was important for the Gospels to show that the Roman governor had believed that Jesus was innocent, but had given way to the pressure of the crowd.

Crucifixion was a Roman punishment, not a Jewish one, and there is no doubt that Jesus was executed on the order of Pontius Pilate, the Roman 'procurator' (governor) of Judaea. Each Gospel claims that Pilate could not find Jesus guilty of any crime. Why, then, did he order his death? Mark says that it was 'to satisfy the crowd', and Luke adds 'they were urgent, demanding with loud cries that he should be crucified. And their voices prevailed.' Matthew suggests that Pilate was afraid that a riot was beginning, and John writes that 'the Jews cried out, "If you release this man your are not Caesar's friend." '

Thus, the Gospels describe Pilate as not strong enough to act upon his own opinion of Jesus, but apart from this they do not blame him. They make it plain that the Jewish crowd wanted Jesus killed, and Mark says that the crowd had been 'stirred up' by the chief priests.

Questions

1 Which Gospel suggests that Pilate expected a riot if he released Jesus?

2 What is meant by 'they were urgent'?

3 Who was Caesar, and why would Pilate not wish to offend him?

4 How could the chief priests 'stir up' the crowd?

5 How did the Gospels show the Romans that Jesus was not a traitor?

How was Jesus questioned by the leaders of the Jewish Church?

The Gospels all agree that Jesus was arrested during the night, and that he was taken to Pilate on the following morning by the leaders of the Jewish Church. What had happened in the meantime? There are three rather different stories.

John writes that Jesus was taken to the house of Annas, a former High Priest, and that he was questioned by him, and then by Caiaphas, the High Priest at that time.

Mark and Matthew say that Jesus was questioned by a large council, once during the night, and again 'as soon as it was morning'. Luke describes one council meeting only, which took place 'when day came'. Probably, these three writers were thinking of the Sanhedrin, the most important Jewish court of law, which had seventy-one members, presided over by the High Priest.

Mark, Luke and Matthew believed that, before the chief priests took him to Pilate, they had decided that Jesus deserved to die. It is most unlikely that the Gospel-writers had any detailed account of what was said during the secret questioning of Jesus, but we know that they were utterly convinced that Jesus was the Son of God. Therefore, it was easy for them to suppose that Jesus had been condemned because he had told the council just this—that he *was* the Son of God.

Here is part of Mark's account (*Mark 14, verses 53–72*):

> 'And they led Jesus to the high priest; and all the chief priests and the elders and scribes were assembled . . . Now the chief priests and the whole council sought testimony against Jesus to put him to death; but they found none. For many bore false witness against him, and their witness did not agree . . . And the high priest stood up in the midst, and asked Jesus, "Have you no answer to make? What is it that these men testify against you?" But he was silent and made no answer. Again the high priest asked him, "Are you the Christ, the Son of the Blessed?" And Jesus said, "I am; and you will see the Son of Man seated at the right hand of Power, and coming with the clouds of heaven." And the high priest tore his mantle, and said, "Why do we still need witnesses? You have heard his blasphemy. What is your decision?" And they all condemned him as deserving death.'

Notes

1 Jews thought it wrong to mention God by name if they could avoid doing so. Therefore 'the Blessed' means God.

2 'The Christ' means 'the anointed one, the Messiah' (*see page 3*).

3 'Blasphemy' means 'abusing the name of God', and the punishment was set out in the Jewish Book of Leviticus (24, verse 16): 'He who blasphemes the name of the Lord shall be put to death; all the congregation shall stone him . . .'

4 When a Jew heard somebody blaspheme, it was his duty to tear his own 'mantle' (outer garment).

A High Priest wearing a mantle

How could it be argued that Jesus was guilty of blasphemy?

The questioning of Jesus is also described by Matthew (*26, verses 57–68*) and by Luke (*22, verses 66–71*). They agree with Mark that the vital questions asked by the High Priest were: 'Are you the Messiah?', 'Are you the Son of God?' We have seen, on page 76, that only Mark suggests that Jesus gave a clear 'I am', but that no writer suggests that he said 'No'. We may assume, then, that the High Priest understood that Jesus had admitted that he was the Messiah. But this did not make him guilty of blasphemy. The Jews thought of the coming Messiah as the greatest of all leaders, but they did not think of him as the Son of God (*see page 74*). Moreover, other Jews had claimed to be the Messiah, and there is no record that any of them had been stoned. To claim to be the Messiah had not been regarded as blasphemy.

According to Mark and Matthew, the High Priest tore his mantle after Jesus had spoken of the Son of Man seated at the right hand of God. If the High Priest thought that this was blasphemy, he must have decided that Jesus was calling himself the Son of Man, and was saying that he would soon be next in importance to God. The Gospel writers had no doubt whatever that Jesus *was* next in importance to God. For them he was the Messiah and the Son of God; and they believed, also, that he had spoken of himself as the Son of Man. Therefore, in writing the questions and answers in their accounts they had shown that Jesus was in no way guilty of the offence for which he was condemned. He had simply told the truth about himself, and for this he had been condemned as a blasphemer. No attempt was made to stone him. He was taken to Pilate, to be killed in another way.

Questions

1 If 'all the chief priests and the elders and the scribes' were first assembled during the night, which of the following is most likely to be true:

a That they just happened to be in the house of the High Priest at that time?

b That they were late going home after another meeting?

c That the meeting had been arranged beforehand, because it was assumed that Jesus would be arrested during the night?

2 What words of Mark suggest that the council had decided on its verdict before Jesus was questioned?

3 If the chief priests had carefully collected witnesses to give false evidence against him, what is surprising about the evidence which they gave?

4 When he gave his answer, what word did Jesus use to refer to God?

The trial before Pilate, *Luke 23, verses 1–5*

'Then the whole company of them arose, and brought him before Pilate. And they began to accuse him, saying, "We found this man perverting our nation, and forbidding us to give tribute to Caesar, and saying that he himself is Christ, a king." And Pilate asked him, "Are you the King of the Jews?" And he answered him, "You have said so." And Pilate said to the chief priests and the multitudes, "I find no crime in this man." But they were urgent, saying, "He stirs up the people, teaching throughout all Judaea, from Galilee even to this place." '

According to Luke, when Pilate heard that Jesus came from Galilee, he sent him to Herod Antipas, the governor of Galilee, who was in Jerusalem at that time, but Herod sent him back to Pilate. The other Gospels do not mention this. The charge that Jesus had forbidden the payment of taxes to Caesar was clearly a false one, as Luke had shown in an earlier passage (*Luke 20, verses 22–25*).

To Pilate, the chief priests made no mention of blasphemy,

because this would not have interested him; but they used the words 'Christ, a king' in such a way as to suggest that Jesus had claimed to be an earthly ruler. They hoped that this would make Pilate agree that Jesus was a danger to the peace of the state, but Pilate was not convinced. Yet he gave way to pressure.

For many years, animals and coins were sold in the outer courts of the Temple. Jesus halted this trading for a short time

Conclusion

According to Mark, Pilate 'perceived that it was out of envy that the chief priests had delivered him up'. Whether Pilate thought this or not, the Gospel-writers certainly believed that the chief priests had been jealous of Jesus, and even afraid of him. They suggested that these were the reasons:

Too many people were attracted by his teaching.

Although he respected the Jewish Law in most ways, his words challenged people to think about their duty to God in a new and disturbing manner.

He said that God loved sinners as well as those who kept strictly to the Law.

He ate meals with people who were known to be dishonest.

He had broken the rules about the Sabbath Day, an offence for which the proper punishment was stoning.

He had entered Jerusalem at the head of a noisy crowd, and his procession might have led to serious disorder.

He had complained bitterly about the normal buying and selling of coins and animals which had gone on for years in the outer courts of the Temple, and he had brought trading to a halt, for a short time at least.

He had often spoken angrily about Pharisees and other strict Jews, suggesting that they were not sincere in what they did, or that they were so much concerned with the details of the Law that they forgot to be kind and generous to their fellow-men.

So the Gospel-writers built up a picture of Jesus going deliberately to Jerusalem, although he knew that he had many enemies, and he had a strong feeling that he would be obliged to die there.

Almost all the blame for what happened is placed upon the Jewish leaders, who are shown as thinking that Jesus was a dangerous threat to their comfortable way of living and teaching.

Perhaps they have been blamed too much. It is impossible now to be sure.

13 What happened after the crucifixion?

If Peter, Paul and others had not been convinced that Jesus appeared and spoke to them after his death, it is more than likely that we would never have heard of Jesus. The letters of Paul would not have been written, and there would have been no 'God-story' or good news for the Gospels to tell.

The earliest written account of these appearances is found in the first letter of Paul to the Corinthians, and part of this was quoted on page 2. Strangely, Paul did not mention several of the appearances which are described in the Gospels, nor did he refer to the stories of the empty tomb. Yet he made it completely clear that he was a Christian because he knew that Jesus had overcome death.

Peter, in his first recorded address to Jews in Jerusalem, spoke in a similar way (*Acts 2*):

> 'this Jesus, delivered up according to the definite plan and foreknowledge of God, you crucified and killed by the hands of lawless men. But God raised him up, having loosed the pangs of death, because it was not possible for him to be held by it . . . and of that we are all witnesses.'

Peter meant that they had seen Jesus after the Resurrection, and he quoted many verses from the Jewish scriptures to try to convince his hearers that all that had happened had been foretold in their Bible.

Jews who followed the teachings of the Pharisees were ready to believe that a body could be resurrected, but they meant by this that the body must be real, not a ghost nor a spirit. Therefore we can imagine them trying to trap Peter and the other disciples with awkward questions:

a How can you prove that you did not imagine the appearance of Jesus after his death?

b How can you prove that his body was not still in the tomb?

c Even if it had gone, how can you prove that you or your friends did not steal it?

d How can you prove that you saw Jesus, and not somebody else?

e Did anybody touch him, to find out if he were real?

The Gospel stories of Easter Day

It is clear that when the Gospel stories were written, there were still several different accounts in the 'tradition' of the Church of what had happened on the first Easter Day.

Mark 16, verses 1–8

'And when the sabbath was past, Mary Magdalene, and Mary the mother of James, and Salome, bought spices, so that they might go and anoint him. And very early on the first day of the week they went to the tomb when the sun had risen. And they were saying to one another, "Who will roll away the stone for us from the door of the tomb?" And looking up, they saw that the stone was rolled back—it was very large. And entering the tomb, they saw a young man sitting on the right side, dressed in a white robe; and they were amazed. And he said to them, "Do not be amazed; you seek Jesus of Nazareth, who was crucified. He has risen, he is not here; see the place where they laid him. But go, tell his disciples and Peter that he is going before you to Galilee; there you will see him, as he told you." And they went out and fled from the tomb; for trembling and astonishment had come upon them; and they said nothing to any one, for they were afraid.'

'Mary Magdalene approaching the sepulchre' by Savoldo

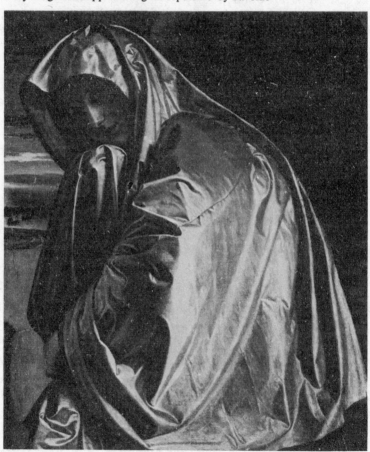

Matthew 27, verses 62–66,
Matthew 28, verses 1–10

'... the chief priests and the Pharisees gathered before Pilate and said, "Sir, we remember how that impostor said, while he was still alive, 'After three days will I rise again.' Therefore order the sepulchre to be made secure until the third day, lest his disciples go and steal him away, and tell the people, 'He has risen from the dead'". ... Pilate said to them, "You have a guard of soldiers; go, make it as secure as you can." So they went and made the sepulchre secure by sealing the stone and setting a guard.

Now after the sabbath, toward the dawn of the first day of the week, Mary Magdalene and the other Mary went to see the sepulchre. And behold, there was a great earthquake; for an angel of the Lord descended from heaven and came and rolled back the stone, and sat upon it. His appearance was like lightning, and his raiment white as snow. And for fear of him the guards trembled and became like dead men. But the angel said to the women, "Do not be afraid, for I know that you seek Jesus who was crucified. He is not here; for he has risen, as he said. Come and see the place where he lay. Then go quickly and tell his disciples that he has risen from the dead, and behold, he is going before you to Galilee; there you will see him." So they departed quickly from the tomb with fear and great joy, and ran to tell his disciples. And behold, Jesus met them and said, "Hail!" And they came up and took hold of his feet and worshipped him. Then Jesus said to them, "Do not be afraid; go and tell my brethren to go to Galilee, and there they will see me."'

Luke 24, verses 1–12

'But on the first day of the week, at early dawn, they went to the tomb, taking the spices which they had prepared. And they found the stone rolled away from the tomb, but when they went in they did not find the body. While they were perplexed about this, behold, two men stood by them in dazzling apparel; and as they were frightened and bowed their faces to the ground, the men said to them, "Why do you seek the living among the dead? Remember how he told you, while he was still in Galilee, that the Son of Man must be delivered into the hands of sinful men, and be crucified, and on the third day rise." And they remembered his words, and returning from the tomb they told all this to the eleven and to all the rest. Now it was Mary Magdalene and Joanna and Mary the mother of James and the other women with them who told this to the apostles; but these words seemed to them an idle tale, and they did not believe them.'

John 20, verses 1–2, 11–18

'Now on the first day of the week Mary Magdalene came to the tomb early, while it was still dark, and saw that the stone had been taken away from the tomb. So she ran, and went to Simon Peter and the other disciple, the one whom Jesus loved, and said to them, "They have taken the Lord out of the tomb, and we do not know where they have laid him'.

John then describes how the two disciples ran to the tomb, saw that it was empty, and then went back to their homes.

'But Mary stood weeping outside the tomb, and as she wept she stooped to look into the tomb; and she saw two angels in white, sitting where the body of Jesus had lain, one at the head and one at the feet. They said to her, "Woman, why are you weeping?" She said to them, "Because they have taken away my Lord, and I do not know where they have laid him." Saying this, she turned round and saw Jesus standing, but she did not know that it was Jesus. Jesus said to her, "Woman, why are you weeping? Whom do you seek?" Supposing him to be the gardener, she said to him, "Sir, if you have carried him away, tell me where you have laid him, and I will take him away." Jesus said to her, "Mary." She turned and said to him in Hebrew "*Rab-boni!*" [*which means Teacher*]. Jesus said to her, "Do not hold me, for I have not yet ascended to the Father; but go to my brethren and say to them, I am ascending to my Father and your Father, to my God and your God." Mary Magdalene went and said to the disciples, "I have seen the Lord."

Questions

1 On page 94 it was suggested that the Jews might have asked the disciples certain questions.
Which Gospel accounts would provide an answer to question *b*?
Which provides an answer to question *c*?
Which provides an answer to question *e*?

2 All the statements below are based upon the Gospels. Look at each statement in turn, and then give the name (or names) of the Gospel (or Gospels) on which it is based. (It may be one Gospel only, or it may be two, three or four.)
a The first visit to the tomb was at sunrise, or even earlier.
b The first visit to the tomb was made by Mary Magdalene, Mary the mother of James, and by Salome.
c Mary Magdalene was one of the first to visit the tomb.
d It was possible to enter the tomb.
e The stone at the entrance was removed by an angel.
f The body of Jesus was not in the tomb.
g The women told nobody what they had seen.
h The women were given a message for the disciples, and ran to give it to them.
i The message was that the disciples would see Jesus in Galilee.

j The disciples (apostles) did not believe the message.
k Jesus appeared, and spoke to two women named Mary.
l At the tomb, Jesus appeared to Mary Magdalene only, and spoke to her.

3 On which of the statements do all four Gospels agree?

Later appearances of Jesus

Two important questions remained:

How could the disciples prove that they had not just seen visions of Jesus?

Even if the person they saw was real, how could they prove that it was Jesus and not somebody else?

Luke deals with both questions in his 24th chapter, but he admits, frankly, that the two disciples whom Jesus joined on the road to Emmaus did not recognize him until just before he left them.

'The Supper at Emmaus' by Caravaggio

Luke 24, verses 13–43

'That very day [Easter Day], two of them [disciples] were going to a village named Emmaus, about seven miles from Jerusalem, and talking with each other about all these things that had happened. While they were talking and discussing together, Jesus himself drew near and went with them. But their eyes were kept from recognizing him. And he said to them, "What is this conversation which you are holding with each other as you walk?" And they stood still, looking sad. Then one of them, named Cleopas, answered him, "Are you the only visitor to Jerusalem who does not know the things that have happened there in these days?" And he said to them, "What things?" And they said to him, "Concerning Jesus of Nazareth, who was a prophet mighty in deed and word before God and all the people, and how our chief priests and rulers delivered him up to be condemned to death, and crucified him. But we had hoped that he was the one to redeem Israel. Yes, and besides all this, it is now the third day since this happened. Moreover, some women of our company amazed us. They were at the tomb early in the morning and did not find his body; and they came back saying that they had even seen a vision of angels, who said that he was alive. Some of those who were with us went to the tomb, and found it just as the women had said; but him they did not see." And he said to them, "O foolish men, and slow of heart to believe all that the prophets have spoken! Was it not necessary that the Christ should suffer these things and enter into his glory?" And beginning with Moses and all the prophets, he interpreted to them in all the scriptures the things concerning himself.

So they drew near to the village to which they were going. He appeared to be going further, but they constrained him, saying, "Stay with us, for it is toward evening and the day is now far spent." So he went in to stay with them. When he was at table with them, he took the bread and blessed, and broke it, and gave it to them. And their eyes were opened and they recognized him; and he vanished out of their sight. They said to each other, "Did not our hearts burn within us while he talked to us on the road, while he opened to us the scriptures?" And they rose that same hour and returned to Jerusalem; and they found the eleven gathered together and those who were with them, who said, "The Lord has risen indeed, and has appeared to Simon!" Then they told what had happened on the road, and how he was known to them in the breaking of the bread.

A rock tomb

As they were saying this, Jesus himself stood among them. But they were startled and frightened, and supposed that they saw a spirit. And he said to them, "Why are you troubled, and why do questionings rise in your hearts? See my hands and my feet, that it is I myself; handle me, and see; for a spirit has not flesh and bones as you see that I have." And while they still disbelieved for joy, and wondered, he said to them, "Have you anything here to eat?" They gave him a piece of broiled fish, and he took and ate before them.'

Questions

1 The men on the road to Emmaus looked sad. Had they believed the reported message of the angels, that Jesus was alive?

2 How does Luke show his belief that everything that happened to Jesus had been foretold in the Jewish scriptures?

3 According to Luke, what evidence showed that the disciples were not seeing a vision or a spirit?
What enabled the disciples to be sure that they were seeing Jesus, and not somebody else?

Conclusion

Matthew 28, verses 16–21, tells how Jesus appeared to eleven disciples in Galilee, 'And when they saw him they worshipped him: but some doubted.'

Mark's Gospel ends after the visit to the tomb. Bible scholars agree that the remainder of chapter 16 was not written by Mark. John gives accounts of three appearances in chapters 20 and 21, and he makes it plain that Thomas, who doubted at first, was completely convinced by a second appearance.

A later appearance, to Saul (Paul), is described three times in the Acts of the Apostles.

Taking all these accounts together, we realize that there is much that we cannot explain, but an historian has no right to say 'I cannot explain this event, therefore it did not happen.' The Gospel writers all belonged to Christian groups which had come into being because certain men and women had been utterly convinced that they had seen and spoken to Jesus, and even eaten with him, after his crucifixion. They had been willing to die rather than to deny what they had seen and heard, and there was no way in which they could have given stronger proof of their sincerity. Their unshakeable belief in the Resurrection is a fact of history which nobody can doubt, and upon it the Christian Church has been built.